Herbert Puchta Günter Gerngross Pe... Lewis-Jones

Super Minds

Student's Book 4

CAMBRIDGE
UNIVERSITY PRESS

Map of the book

Well done, Ben and Lucy! (pages 4–9)

Vocabulary	Grammar	Story Phonics
At town events	Do you / Does Lucy like (reading)? When do you start (school)? What was in (the book)? How did you find (the book)?	The map Rhyming words

▶ **Song:** The Explorers

① In the museum (pages 10–21)

Vocabulary	Grammar	Story Phonics	Skills and value	Thinking skills	English for school
Knights and queens	I must (wear a helmet). I mustn't (swim here). Give me / him / her / us / them (the book), please.	The knight The letter sound ow	• Reading The secret of the Egyptian cat • Applying what you know	• Using one's imagination	**History:** Discover museums

▶ **Song:** It's midnight ▶ **Creativity** ▶ **Revision**

② The world around us (pages 22–33)

Vocabulary	Grammar	Story Phonics	Skills and value	Thinking skills	English for school
The countryside	but, and, because, so I could / couldn't (run 20 kilometres). Could you (swim for 10 hours)?	At the restaurant Silent consonants	• Reading • Listening and writing • Making time for the family	• Finding alternative ideas • Time sequencing • Sequencing pictures	**Art:** Life in art

▶ **Song:** Walking with Mum ▶ **Creativity** ▶ **Revision**

③ Danger! (pages 34–45)

Vocabulary	Grammar	Story Phonics	Skills and value	Thinking skills	English for school
Emergencies	I was / We were (climbing a tree). What was she / were they doing? Was he / Were we (playing)? Yes, he was. / No, he wasn't. Yes, we were. / No, we weren't.	The man in the car The sound /aɪ/	• Reading The day the sea went out • Responding to emergencies	• Finding alternative ideas • Developing deduction skills	**Human health and safety:** Fire safety

▶ **Song:** Yesterday at half past nine ▶ **Creativity** ▶ **Revision**

④ Two return tickets (pages 46–57)

Vocabulary	Grammar	Story Phonics	Skills	Thinking skills	English for school and value
At the train station	in (September), at (one o'clock), on (Sunday), in the (morning) I was (having dinner) when you phoned me.	The tunnel The sound /eə/	• Reading • Listening and speaking	• Interpreting sentences • Developing research skills • Judging information	**Science:** Forces Using force carefully

▶ **Song:** Mr Knocks ▶ **Creativity** ▶ **Revision**

⑤ Police! (pages 58–69)

Vocabulary	Grammar	Story Phonics	Skills and value	Thinking skills	English for school
Hair and face	He used to (be a police officer). We had to (be really careful).	The Mysterious H The sounds /ɑː/ and /ɔː/	• Reading Yatin and the orange tree • Being honest	• Paying attention to visual details • Processing information	**Literature:** Crime fiction

▶ **Song:** Who are you?   ▶ **Creativity**   ▶ **Revision**

⑥ Mythical beasts (pages 70–81)

Vocabulary	Grammar	Story Phonics	Skills	Thinking skills	English for school and value
Animal bodies	longer / more dangerous than better / worse than the biggest / heaviest / most dangerous the best / worst What does (a unicorn) look like? It looks like (a horse).	The secret door The letter sound ea	• Listening • Speaking and writing	• Logical thinking, categorising • Thinking creatively • Developing information processing skills	**Science:** Protection Appreciating nature

▶ **Song:** The most beautiful dinosaur   ▶ **Creativity**   ▶ **Revision**

⑦ Orchestra practice (pages 82–93)

Vocabulary	Grammar	Story Phonics	Skills and value	Thinking skills	English for school
Instruments	mine, yours, his, hers, ours, theirs Connor's the boy who … The instrument which … The house where …	At the concert hall The sounds /ɜː/ and /ɔː/	• Reading The bear's dream • Enjoying being different	• Summarising • Reasoning • Empathising • Making hypotheses	**Science in Music:** How we make sounds

▶ **Song:** Chaos in the classroom   ▶ **Creativity**   ▶ **Revision**

⑧ In the planetarium (pages 94–105)

Vocabulary	Grammar	Story Phonics	Skills and value	Thinking skills	English for school
Space	What will you be when you grow up? I'll be a (police officer). badly, carefully, quickly, quietly, slowly	The trap Word stress and the sound /ə/	• Listening and reading • Speaking and writing • Respecting your elders	• Observation and deduction • Analysing data	**Science:** The solar system

▶ **Song:** One day I'll be an astronaut   ▶ **Creativity**   ▶ **Revision**

⑨ At the campsite (pages 106–117)

Vocabulary	Grammar	Story Phonics	Skills and value	Thinking skills	English for school
Holiday activities	some cheese / tomatoes, a loaf of bread, a piece of cheese, a packet of crisps, a bottle of milk, a can of lemonade. How much cheese / How many bottles of water … ?	The last line Unstressed words	• Reading The snares in the forest • Protecting wildlife	• Identifying relevant information • Developing visual-spatial thinking	**Geography:** Map reading

▶ **Song:** We're going on a picnic   ▶ **Creativity**   ▶ **Revision**

Grammar focus: pages 118–127

Well done, Ben and Lucy!

CD1 02 Listen and say the words. Then check with a friend.

1 big wheel
2 rollercoaster
3 roundabout
4 mayor
5 dodgem cars
6 microphone
7 band
8 photographer
9 journalist

WELL DONE, BEN AND LUCY!

CD1 03 Listen and answer.

1 Where are Ben and Lucy?

2 Why are they there?

3 Who wants to talk to Ben and Lucy?

4 What does Lucy want to do first?

Play the secret word game.

My secret word works for a newspaper.

A journalist!

You speak into my secret word.

A microphone!

CD 1 04 **Listen and circle.**

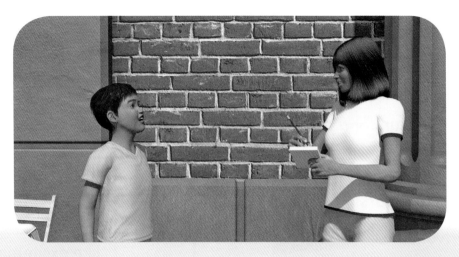

1	Do you like going on adventures?	a	Yes, I love it.	b	No, I hate it.
2	Do you want to be famous?	a	Yes, I do.	b	No, I don't.
3	What do you want to be when you're older?	a	An explorer.	b	A librarian.
4	What do you like doing in your free time?	a	Playing computer games.	b	Reading books.
5	Is Lucy your best friend?	a	Yes, she is.	b	No, she isn't.
6	Does Lucy like Buster?	a	Yes, she does.	b	No, she doesn't.

 CD 1 05 **Grammar focus** **Listen and say.**

Do you **like** going to school?

Where do you **live**?

Does Lucy **like** reading books?

When do you **start** school?

Are you **brave**?

Is your life exciting?

Interview a friend. Find out four new things.

Do you want to be famous?

What colour are the walls in your room?

What time do you … ?

What's your favourite … ?

Ben	Lucy	
		likes adventure.
		likes exploring.
		isn't scared of anything.
		finds lots of treasure.
		like excitement.

The Explorers.
Here they come.
Lucy and Ben. Adventure and fun.
The Explorers.
Here they are.
Ben and Lucy. Action stars.

Does Ben like adventure?
Yes, he does.
He loves exploring things
Just like us.

The Explorers ...

Is Lucy scared of anything?
No, she's not.
Does she find much treasure?
Yes, a lot.

The Explorers ...

Do they like excitement?
Yes, they do.
Here's their next adventure.
You can join in too!

The Explorers ...

2 CD1 07 **Listen and sing.**

3 **What do you like or love doing? Tell a friend.**

I like having fun with my friends.

I love walking in the mountains.

1 Complete the interview. Listen and check.

school   clues   castle
door   statue   librarian

Journalist: So, Lucy, tell me about your adventure. How did you find the (1) _____ ?

Lucy: It all started when we found an old book in the castle.

Journalist: What was in the book?

Lucy: It had a secret code. We needed to break the code and then we used it to read the clues.

Journalist: What did the (2) _____ do?

Lucy: They helped us to find letters.

Journalist: And what did the letters do?

Lucy: We used the letters to make a word. With this word we opened a (3) _____ in the (4) _____ and found the treasure.

Journalist: Was it dangerous?

Lucy: Yes, it was. There were two 'baddies': a man called Horax and a woman called Zelda.

Journalist: Did they want the book?

Lucy: Yes, they wanted the book to find the treasure. They wanted to keep it and we found out later that Horax was our school (5) _____ , Mr Williams. We were shocked.

Journalist: Oh no! Does he still work at your (6) _____ ?

Lucy: No, he doesn't. We don't know where he is now.

2  **Listen and say.**

Was it dangerous?

What was in the book?

Were you scared?

How did you **find** the statue?

Did they **want** the book?

3 **Play the guessing game.**

Guess what I did in the holidays.

No, I didn't.

Did you do a lot of sports?

Did you go to the beach a lot?

The map

1

Mr Davidson: Mmm, it really is a beautiful statue. It's very, very old.
Lucy: We had an amazing adventure to find it.
Ben: It was exciting and quite dangerous too.

2

Mr Davidson: This symbol here … I know this …
Lucy: What is it?
Mr Davidson: That's it! Now I remember. Wait here a moment.

3

Ben: Very strange. *What* does he remember?
Lucy: And where did he go? Into the museum?
Ben: I think so. But what's that symbol?

4

Mr Davidson: Here you are. Look at this.
Lucy: What is it?
Mr Davidson: A map from the museum.

5

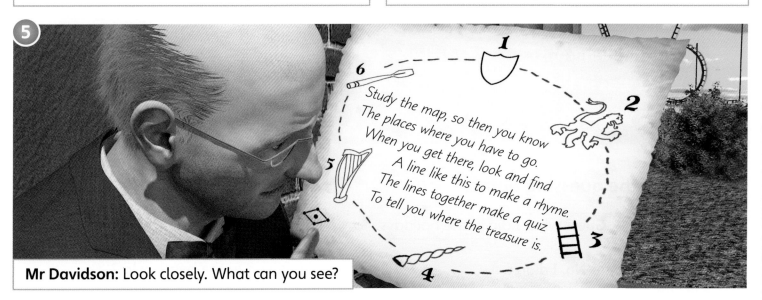

Study the map, so then you know
The places where you have to go.
When you get there, look and find
A line like this to make a rhyme.
The lines together make a quiz
To tell you where the treasure is.

Mr Davidson: Look closely. What can you see?

6

Ben: The symbol! It's the same as on the statue.
Mr Davidson: This diamond is the symbol of an old English king. With this map you can find more of the king's treasure.

7

Horax: Zelda, it's me. The kids have got a treasure map.
Zelda: We have to follow them and find the treasure before they do.

2 Answer the questions.

1 What does Mr Davidson find on the statue?

2 Where does he go?

3 What does he get?

4 What do Ben and Lucy have to make to find the treasure?

5 Who is watching them?

6 What are Horax and Zelda going to do?

3 Find the train and the plane in the story.

4 CD 1 12 **Listen and say.**

The boys can make noise, but Sue can too!

1 In the museum

CD 1 14 **Listen and say the words. Then check with a friend.**

1 queen
2 knight
3 crown
4 helmet
5 necklace
6 bracelet
7 belt
8 shield
9 bow and arrow
10 sword

CD 1 15 **Listen and correct the sentences.**

1 There is a helmet on the map.
2 Ben is talking about the helmet.
3 Lucy would like the queen's crown.
4 They go to the dinosaur room.

Ask and answer.

Where's the sword?
The knight's carrying it.

Where's the bracelet?
The queen's wearing it.

1 Look, read and number the sentences.

a I must buy a ticket. ☐
b I must put my dog on a lead. ☐
c I must leave my coat in the cloakroom. ☐
d I must speak quietly. ☐
e I mustn't shout. ☐
f I mustn't run. ☐
g I mustn't touch anything. ☐
h I mustn't take photos. ☐

2 CD 1 16 Grammar focus Listen and say.

I **must wear** a helmet.   I **mustn't swim** here.

3 Play the *mustn't forget* game.

Wash up.   That's right. I mustn't forget to wash up.

1 CD 1 17 **Listen to the song. Number the pictures.**

It's a museum ... I mustn't dance, I mustn't fight,
I mustn't shout ... but at midnight ...

It's midnight. It's midnight.
Take a look at the clock.
Come on, let's rock!
Come on, let's rock!

Bracelets, crowns are flying round,
Necklaces are on the ground.
Here comes our dinosaur.
There are kings and queens and more.
It's midnight ...

Statues dance and lions roar.
Crash! The vase is on the floor.
The swords then shout, 'Come on, let's fight!
Let's fight all night until it's light.'
It's midnight ...

Yeah!

2 CD 1 18 **Listen and sing.**

3 **Make word chains.**

g r o u n d i n o s a u r o a r

CD 1 19 Complete the sentences. Listen and check.

necklace   coats   crown   swords   shield

1

Give us the
_____ , please.

2

Give him the
_____ , please.

3

Give me the
_____ , please.

4

Give her the
_____ , please.

5

Give them the
_____ , please.

2 CD 1 20 Grammar focus Listen and say.

Give **me the book**, please.
Give **him the camera**, please.
Give **them the sandwiches**, please.

Give **her the apple**, please.
Give **us the pencils**, please.

3 Play the *Show me* game.

Show me the necklace.

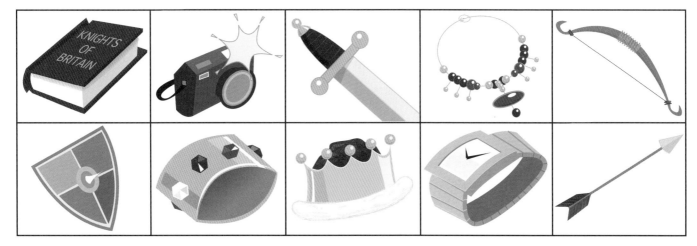

The knight

Lucy: Now, let's look for the first line of the rhyme.
Ben: I really hope we can find it here.

Ben: Help! That was close!
Lucy: Where did it come from?
Ben: I don't know, but someone is trying to hurt us.

Ben: I can't see anyone.
Lucy: Look, there's a knight with a sword. He's coming after us. Let's run.

Ben: Look, this is a good place to hide.
Lucy: I hope the knight doesn't find us.
Ben: Shhh. We mustn't make a noise.

Lucy: I've got an idea. Hold the lead. Buster, come here!
Ben: That's it, Buster! Good dog!

Ben: That was a brilliant idea.
Lucy: I'm glad it worked. I was very scared.

Ben: Look! The knight's shield! It's the first symbol! And there's the line of the rhyme.
Lucy: Let me see. 'Behind the picture in the frame.' We must write it down.

Zelda: Poor Horax. How do you feel?
Horax: Terrible! I'm going to get those children.
Zelda: And their map.

2 Answer the questions.

Who …

1 sees the knight first?
2 finds a place to hide?
3 is on a lead?
4 has a brilliant idea?
5 sees the shield?
6 doesn't feel very well?

3 Find the crown and the arrow in the story.

CD1 22 Listen and say.

A crowd watched the clown show from the window.

1 Read the story quickly. Who knows the secret?

CD 1
25 Read and listen. Check your answer.

The secret of the Egyptian cat

Mr Benson was the director of a small museum in a town in England. He loved his museum. When groups of children visited, he took them around and showed them all the things in the museum. He told them interesting stories and the children enjoyed visiting his museum.

There was one object that Mr Benson loved more than the others. It was a statue of a gold cat from Egypt. It was his best piece and it was very, very old. It was in a glass case and, of course, there was an alarm.

When Mr Benson arrived at the museum in the morning, he always went to look at the statue of the gold cat. When he left the museum in the evening, Mr Benson locked all the windows and doors. He then said goodbye to the cat and he went home to have dinner with his wife and his eighteen-year-old daughter, Cleo.

One night Mr Benson went to a party with his wife. Mr Benson and his wife were on their way home in their car when the clock struck twelve. They were just next to the museum. A cat ran across the street and Mr Benson stopped the car quickly. 'That was close,' he said.

At that moment his wife said, 'Look, there's a window open at the museum.' 'That's strange, I must go and close it,' said Mr Benson. They went home quickly, he got the key, went back to the museum and closed the window. And then he saw that the statue of the gold cat was not in the glass case any more. He checked the alarm, but it was fine. He called the police and they came to the museum. Mr Benson told them all about the cat and he wrote a report.

The next morning, he told Cleo about the missing statue of the gold cat and also about the cat in the street near the museum. Cleo went with her dad to the museum and checked the glass case again. There was no gold cat. The alarm was still on.

'Which window was open?' Cleo asked. Her dad showed her the window.

'Let me stay at the museum tonight,' Cleo said to her dad. 'I've got an idea. I read a book about the secrets of Egyptian cats.'

Her dad wasn't happy about Cleo spending the night in the museum, but he said yes. In the evening Cleo went to the museum with a torch. Just before midnight she opened the same window and waited. She couldn't see anything but she heard a little noise. She waited a minute and then switched on the torch. Yes – the case was empty! An hour after midnight she heard a noise again. She waited a minute and then she switched on the torch. The gold cat was in the glass case. Cleo closed the window and went to the glass case.

'I hope you had some fun outside,' she said to the gold cat. 'Dad isn't going to forget to close a window again.'

 Answer the questions.

1 Who was Mr Benson?

2 What did Mr Benson and his wife do one night?

3 Why did Mr Benson stop the car on their way home?

4 Why did Mr Benson go back to the museum?

5 What did he find?

6 What did Cleo do before midnight?

 Think! **Work in pairs. What do you think the cat did?**

He went to visit his friend in another museum.

Then he went fishing.

 **Learn and think**

Discover museums

1 **Read about two museums. Which is the oldest thing in the text?**

a

MUSEO NACIONAL DE ANTROPOLOGIA

The National Museum of Anthropology in Mexico City has the largest collection of ancient Mexican pieces in the world, in 23 galleries. In the museum you can find wonderful exhibits of Aztec culture. The Aztecs lived in central Mexico and ruled a great part of it in the 14th, 15th and 16th centuries. One of the most famous exhibits in the museum is the Sun Stone. It was the calendar of the Aztecs. Another important exhibit is the mask of the Zapotecs. They lived in the south of Mexico and this mask is about 2,000 years old.

b

The Egyptian Museum in Cairo is the most famous museum in Egypt. It has a huge collection of more than 120,000 exhibits and there is a Royal Mummy Room with 27 mummies. When an important person died in ancient Egypt, people treated the body with chemicals and wrapped it in bandages. The Egyptians also put food and jewels with their mummies to give the dead people something to eat and wear in their next life. The most important exhibit in the museum is the gold mask of the Egyptian king Tutankhamun, who lived about 2,700 years ago.

2 **Match the photos with the museums. Write *A* or *B*.**

1 2 3 4

1 **Complete the table about the museums on page 18.**

	A: (1) _____	B: (6) _____
Name of museum:		
Location (City/Country):	(2) _____	(7) _____
Famous collection which you can find there:	(3) _____	(8) _____
Has exhibits about this ancient culture:	(4) _____	(9) _____
Famous exhibits which you can see there:	(5) _____	(10) _____

2 **Work in groups. Ask and answer. Make notes.**

Do you know a museum? Where is it? What's your favourite exhibit?

	museum	city	favourite exhibit(s)
Lucía	Interactive Science Museum	Buenos Aires	Music gallery

3 **Tell the class.**

Lucía knows the Interactive Science Museum in Buenos Aires. Her favourite exhibits are in the Music gallery.

4 Project **Make a collage for a time capsule.**

1 A time capsule contains interesting objects which tell people in the **future** about life in the **past**. Imagine you are making a time capsule. Write a list of four things.

a mobile phone
a computer game
a rucksack
a digital camera

2 Make a collage with photos or drawings.

Act out

A visit from the cat

1 **Choose a role card. Read and plan.**

STUDENT A

You are the Egyptian cat statue from the story. One night your friend comes to see you at the museum. Talk to him / her about:

- your friends at the museum
- Mr Benson
- what you do in the museum
- your favourite exhibits

STUDENT B

You are a cat living near the museum. One night you go to visit your friend at the museum. Ask her questions about her life there. You want her to:

- tell you about her friends at the museum
- tell you about Mr Benson
- tell you what she does
- show you her favourite exhibits

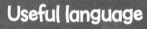

Useful language

Friend	**Cat**
Who are your friends at the museum?	My best friends are …
Is Mr Benson nice?	He's …
What do you do … ?	At night I …
Show me your favourite exhibit. What is it?	My favourite exhibit …

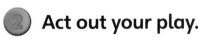

2 **Act out your play.**

Who are your friends at the museum?

My best friend is the knight.

my scrapbook

A museum advert

1 Start a new scrapbook for this year. Write your profile.

My name:
My class:
My teacher's name:
People in my family:
My favourite sport:
My favourite music:
My favourite food and drink:

2 You are going to make an advert. Visit a museum or find out about it on the Internet. Make notes.

Name of museum:	Museum in the Park
What you can learn:	History of Woodville
Exhibits	Old photos, ancient jewellery
Opening hours:	Mon–Fri 9 a.m. – 4 p.m.
Other facts:	Café, shop (books, key rings, postcards, posters)

3 Read the advert. What makes it boring? How could you make it better?

Come to Woodville and visit our interesting museum

It's called the Museum in the Park. Come here to learn interesting things about the history of our town. There are lots of interesting photos in the museum. They show life in our town a long time ago. The most important exhibit is an interesting collection of ancient jewellery. The Museum in the Park is open from 9 a.m. to 4 p.m. There is also a nice café and a shop where you can buy interesting books, key rings, postcards and posters.

4 Make your advert. How many adjectives are there in it?

2 The world around us

1 **Listen and say the words. Then check with a friend.**

1. mountain
2. forest
3. village
4. lake
5. island
6. field
7. river
8. path

2 **Listen and answer.**

1. Why isn't Ben ready to walk?
2. Why is Buster barking?
3. Where are they going next?
4. How long will it take?

3   **Play *I spy*.**

> I spy, with my little eye, something with a 't' in it.

> Is it 'path'?

CD 1 30

Listen, read and write *yes* or *no*.

Ryan: Tell me your story about Sunday.
Sophie: Well, it was a sunny day so we went to Otter Lake and we had a picnic.
Ryan: And?
Sophie: Then after the picnic I went swimming because the water was warm.
Ryan: You had a picnic and went swimming. What happened then?
Sophie: Well, Billy was scared of the fish in the lake, so he didn't go in.
Ryan: I see. Billy didn't go in, but you did because you weren't afraid.
Sophie: That's right. But … a fish bit me.

Ryan: No!
Sophie: Yes. I jumped out of the water. I wasn't afraid, but I was angry because everyone laughed when I told them about the fish. They didn't believe me!
Ryan: Was the fish big?
Sophie: I didn't see it, but I think it was really big.

1 Sophie and her family had a picnic in the forest. _____

2 Sophie went swimming in the lake. _____

3 Billy went swimming with Sophie. _____

4 Sophie jumped out of the water because it was cold. _____

 CD 1 31 **Grammar focus** **Listen and say.**

> I looked into the water, **but** I didn't see the fish.
> We went to a lake **and** we had a picnic there.
> I went swimming **because** the water was warm.
> We were hungry, **so** we went to a restaurant.

  Think! **Make sentences.**

I had a sandwich	because …
I didn't go to the party	so …
We didn't win	and …
I went to bed early	but …

(I went to bed early and I read a book.) (I went to bed early because …)

1 **Listen and tick (✓) the correct pictures.**

Walking with Mum
Is so much fun.
Walking with Mum
In the morning sun.

We got up very early.
What a lovely day!
We walked through some villages,
Singing all the way.

'Let's sit here,' said Mum
And pointed to some trees.
'We can have a picnic –
I've got some bread and cheese.'
Walking with Mum …

We walked through the fields,
But that was a mistake.
Mum didn't see the path
And fell into the lake!

The water was so cold,
Mum's face was blue
And so she caught a cold.
Atchoo! Atchoo!
Walking with Mum …

 2 **Listen and sing.**

3 **Correct the sentences.**

1   The weather wasn't good.
2   They walked through the forest.
3   They ate eggs and tomatoes.
4   A child fell into the water.

 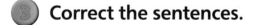

1 CD 1 34 **Listen and number the pictures.**

When I was a young man forty years ago …

a b c

d e f

  2 CD 1 35 **Grammar focus** **Listen and say.**

When I was young 40 years ago I **could jump** higher than a tree.
Could you **swim** for 10 hours?
I **couldn't run** 20 kilometres.

3 **Tell stories about your grandpa or grandma.**

My grandpa could kick a ball five kilometres!

1

Lucy: What a nice restaurant!
Ben: Look at our treasure map, Grandpa.
Grandpa: Oh yes! Ah, but here's our soup. Let's look at the map after lunch.

2

Grandpa: So, it's a treasure map. What are you looking for?
Lucy: There are pictures on the map. We have to find these pictures and the lines of a rhyme.

3

Waiter: Here's your bread.
Lucy: The next picture on the map is a lion. Maybe the next line is at the zoo.
Ben: But you don't find *red* lions at the zoo!

4

Ben: Oh no! The map!
Lucy: What is it?
Ben: It isn't in my pocket and it isn't on the floor.

5

Grandpa: Ben, Lucy … did you want this?
Ben: But where … how did you get that?
Grandpa: You must be more careful!

6

Grandpa: There was something strange about that waiter. I put a menu in your pocket and kept the map. The waiter took the menu.

7

Grandpa: Hmm, that waiter looked like a man that I knew a long time ago. I can tell you later, but first I want to talk about this picture of the red lion.

8

Lucy: The Red Lion! It's this restaurant!
Grandpa: Yes, and now look at the menu.
Ben: It's the symbol and the line! It says: 'Lots of stairs. Climb thirty-three!'

2 **Think!** **Put the story in order.**

- [ ] Ben and Lucy show the map to Grandpa.
- [ ] Grandpa asks the children about the map.
- [ ] Grandpa shows Ben and Lucy the map.
- [ ] The waiter brings the bread.
- [ ] Grandpa helps them to find the line.
- [ ] Ben can't find the map.

3 **Find the sword in the story.**

4 CD1 37 **Listen and say.**

A rhino writing a rescue sign on an island

1 **Read the story. Choose a word from the box.**
Write the correct word next to numbers 1–6.

| apple | banana | bus | car | hour |
| house | river | forest | restaurant | minute |

Last month my parents and I went for a walk. First we drove for an hour and then we parked the (1) _____ . Next we walked through a (2) _____ and saw nothing but trees for two hours. Then we walked another hour to the top of a mountain. We sat down and looked around. Then Mum said to Dad, 'Can you give me a sandwich and an (3) _____ ?' Dad put his hand in the rucksack and looked sad. Mum and I looked at Dad. He couldn't find any sandwiches. 'I'm sorry,' he said, 'I think they're on the table in the kitchen.' Mum and I weren't happy.

We were very hungry. 'I've got an idea,' Dad said. 'We'll go down a different way, to the lake. Near the lake there's a village and there's a good restaurant there.' We stood up and started to go down. When we came to a small (4) _____ , we had to take off our shoes and socks to get to the other side. After two hours, we got to the lake and then we saw the village. We walked over, but there wasn't a (5) _____ in the village. 'Where is our car, Dad?' I asked. 'Well, I think it's only an (6) _____ away.' he answered.

2 **Now choose the best name for the story.**

☐ A mountain walk   ☐ A day without food   ☐ The village without a restaurant

 **Skills**

 CD 1 41

Listen and write the names under the pictures.

> Jack Vicky John Mary Sally

① _____ ② _____

③

④ _____ ⑤ _____

CD 1 42 **Listen again and write *yes* or *no*.**

1 Mary has got a pony. _____
2 Sally likes swimming. _____
3 Jack likes football
   and table tennis. _____

4 Vicky likes picnics. _____
5 John lives in a village. _____
6 Jack likes hiking. _____

 Write about your favourite place.

| Where? | Why? | What do you do there? |

My favourite place is the beach near my house because it's quiet.
I like watching the birds and sometimes I take food for them.

LIFE IN ART

1 **Think!** Look at the paintings. Number them from the oldest (1) to the most recent (4).

W

X

Y

Z

2 Number the topics to match the paintings.

Work ☐   Animals ☐   Nature ☐   Free time ☐

1 Read and write *t* (true) or *f* (false).

Painting W is by Georges Seurat. He painted the picture in 1886. It is a wonderful day near a river in France. The people are outside to enjoy the sunshine. Some of the ladies have parasols because they don't want to get too much sun.

Painting X is from a cave in France. The painters did the painting about 20,000 years ago. They painted the animals which they hunted.

Painting Y is *El Mercado*. It is a modern painting from Mexico. Three women are selling flowers or vegetables at a market. The colours are very bright.

Painting Z is a landscape painting by Joris van der Haagen. He lived in Holland and painted it in about the year 1650. In the foreground there are darker colours. The background with the clouds and the sky is bright. The trees and the river are very realistically painted.

1 The oldest painting shows animals. ☐

2 The painter who did the painting with the quiet river and the trees lived in France. ☐

3 Georges Seurat lives in England. ☐

4 The modern painting is from Mexico. ☐

2 Project Make a *My world* collage.

1 Think of your environment: your family and friends, free time and school.

2 Find photos, draw a picture or create artwork for each item.

3 Write a note for each item on your collage.

3 Present your collage to the class.

My collage shows my house and the river near it, my pets, my friend …

How we spend our free time

1 How many students in your class prefer being …
… outdoors?　　… in town?　　… at home?

Outdoors	In town	At home
✓✓✓✓✓✓✓✓	✓✓✓✓✓	✓✓✓

2 Work in groups (outdoors, town and home). Ask about favourite activities. Make a chart.

> What do you like to do outdoors?

> What do you like to do in town?

> What do you like to do at home?

Outdoors	In town	At home
Ride bike ✓✓✓	Museum ✓	Computer ✓✓
Walk ✓✓	Shopping ✓✓✓	TV ✓

3 Tell the class about your group.

> In the outdoors group, three students like riding their bike …

4 Write a report.

My classmates and their free time

Today we asked what the students in our class prefer doing in their free time. The results were very interesting.

There are 16 students in the class. Half of them (8 students) say that they love being outdoors in their free time. They love riding their bikes (3), going for walks (2) and playing football (3).

5 students (4 girls and 1 boy) prefer hanging out in town. They love going to museums, shopping and going to the cinema.

2 of our classmates spend all their free time in front of computers.

My favourite outdoor place

1 **Read Joshua's description and answer the questions.**

My favourite outdoor place is my grandma's garden. I like it because there are lots of trees and flowers. It's a very quiet garden. I often sit under my favourite apple tree and listen to the birds. My little sister likes the garden too, but she's very noisy so the birds fly away.

1 Where is Joshua's favourite outdoor place?

2 Why does he like it so much?

3 What does he do when he sits under his favourite tree?

4 Why is his little sister a problem in the garden?

2 **Underline *and*, *because*, *but* and *so* in Joshua's text.**

3 **Join the sentences.**

1 I like the river — I love watching the fish in it. — **so**

2 On Sundays my mum and I often go to the forest — we have a picnic. — **because**

3 My best friend lives near a lake — I go swimming with his family in the summer. — **but**

4 I like the park very much — on Sundays there are too many people there. — **and**

4 **Write about your favourite outdoor place. Use the words from Activity 3.**

- Where's your favourite outdoor place?
- Why do you like it?
- What do you like so much about it?
- What do you do there?

③ Danger!

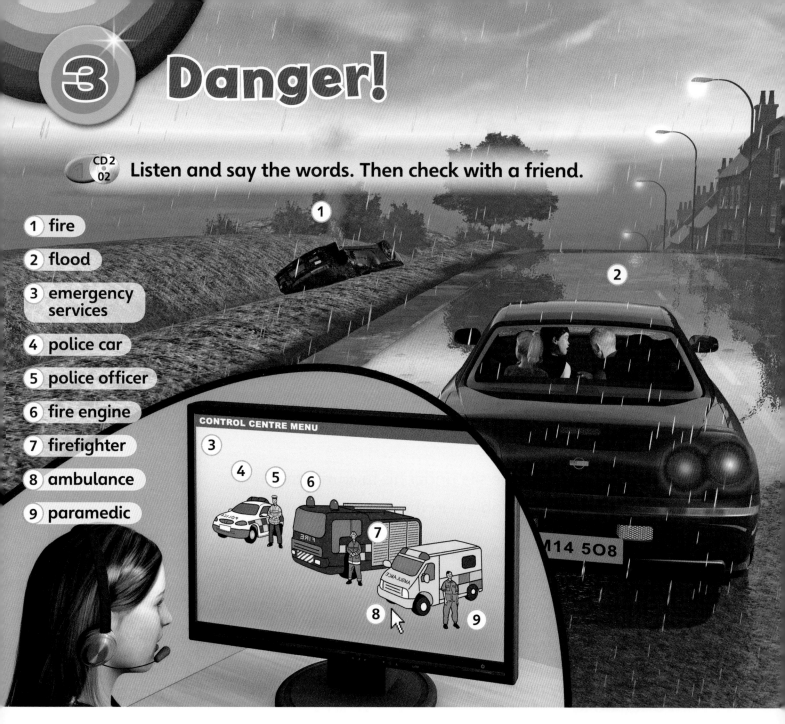

CD 2 02 **Listen and say the words. Then check with a friend.**

1. fire
2. flood
3. emergency services
4. police car
5. police officer
6. fire engine
7. firefighter
8. ambulance
9. paramedic

CONTROL CENTRE MENU

CD 2 03 **Listen and correct the sentences.**

1 The children know Grandpa's story.
2 Grandpa has an accident.
3 A woman's car is on fire.
4 Lucy phones the emergency services.

Make short dialogues. Use the words from Activity 1.

999. Emergency Services. How can I help you?

There's a flood in Green Street. Can you send a boat …

1 **Guess the picture for each sentence. Listen and check.**

a We were running around the swimming pool. ☐

b I was driving very fast. ☐

c I was climbing a tree. ☐

d We were riding our bikes. ☐

2  **Grammar focus** **Listen and say.**

I **was climbing** a tree.
My friend **was swimming** in the pool.
You **were reading** a book.

He **was driving** very fast.
We **were playing** tennis.
They **were riding** bikes.

3 **Complete the sentences.**

When the phone rang,

1 Ella ...

2 Jack ...

3 Holly ...

4 Charlie ...

Past continuous 35

CD2 06 **Listen and complete the song with *was* and *were*.**

Yesterday at half past nine
We (1)_____ having a really great time.
All of my family were at home –
It was fun and we were fine.

Mum (2)_____ feeling very hungry.
She (3)_____ eating a banana cake.
My sister Emily was thirsty, so
She (4)_____ drinking a vanilla shake.

I've got a telescope in my room.
I (5)_____ looking at a big, bright star.
My brother Jonathan was in the hall.
He (6)_____ playing with his new red car.

But just then at half past ten ...
BANG! And all the lights went out.
'Just a little accident,' said my dad,
But everybody started to shout.

'My banana cake!' 'My vanilla shake!'
'Hey, where's Dad?' 'Dad, where are you?'
'Ouch, my telescope!' 'Ow, my car!'
'Here I am!' 'Dad ... was that you?'

CD2 07 **Listen and sing.**

3 **Make sentences.**

At half past nine Emily was
drinking a vanilla shake.

Mum ...

Jonathan ...

I ...

Dad ...

CD 2 08 **Look, read and number the dialogues. Listen and check.**

a 'What were you doing yesterday afternoon?'
   'I was taking the dog for a walk.'

b 'What was she doing at four?' 'She was reading a book.'

c 'Was he watching TV yesterday evening?' 'Yes, he was.'

d 'Were they listening to mp3 players?' 'No, they weren't.'

 CD 2 09 **Grammar focus** **Listen and say.**

What **were** you **doing** yesterday?	I **was watching** TV.
Were they **playing** table tennis?	Yes, they **were**.
Were they **singing**?	No, they **weren't**.
What **was** he **doing** at 4 o'clock?	He **was reading** a book.
Was she **listening** to music?	No, she **wasn't**.
Was he **watching** a film?	Yes, he **was**.

Ask and answer about yesterday.

What were you doing at 4 o'clock?   I was doing my homework.

Were you doing your English homework?   Yes, I was.

Was your brother playing football at 4 o'clock?   No, he wasn't.

What was he doing?   He was watching TV.

The man in the car

1

Grandpa: Take the phone, Lucy. I'm going to help that man.
Ben: Can I come with you, Grandpa?
Grandpa: No way. Stay in the car, please.

2

Lucy: My friend's grandpa has got a fire extinguisher and he's going to help the man in the car.
Operator: Good, but *you* mustn't get out, OK?

3

Operator: Now, Mill Road is a long road. Can you see the number on a house from the car?
Lucy: Yes, I can. We're in front of number 92.

4

Operator: All right. Just wait a few more minutes for the ambulance and the fire engine.
Lucy: I think I can hear the ambulance now!

5

Ben: Wow! Look at Grandpa!
Lucy: He's fantastic!

6

Grandpa: Quick! We must get you out.
Man: Agh, my leg!

Man: I wasn't driving very fast, but suddenly there was this flood …
Grandpa: Hey, you on the motorbike! Don't go so fast! (*He thinks*) Hmm. It's him again.

Lucy: You were fantastic. You saved the man's life!
Ben: And now tell us the story, Grandpa!
Grandpa: Another time. I'm too tired now.

2 Read and make sentences.

1	Ben's grandpa and the children	a	and the car was on fire.
2	Suddenly they saw	b	because he was too tired.
3	A man was in the car	c	were driving in the rain.
4	Grandpa and Lucy talked to	d	to get out of the car.
5	Grandpa helped the man	e	an accident.
6	Grandpa couldn't tell them the story	f	the emergency services.

3 Find the bike and the lights in the story.

4 Listen and say.

Oh Sue!
I love you!
Oh please –
Love me too!

A knight in bright tights writes rhymes by candlelight.

Read the text quickly and try to find the answers.

1 What's the name of the girl?

2 Where was she with her parents?

3 Why was she scared?

Read and listen. Check your answers.

The day the sea went out

It was December 26th, 2004. Tilly Smith, a ten-year-old girl from England, was on holiday in Thailand with her parents. Together with her parents and hundreds of other tourists, she was enjoying the sea and the sun on the beautiful Maikhao Beach near Phuket in the south of Thailand.

It was eight o'clock in the morning. Tilly and her parents were in the water, playing with a ball. Tilly looked around. Lots of people were at the beach and they were having fun. Some were swimming and snorkelling. Two boys were trying to catch fish. A boy and a girl were building a sandcastle. Other people were reading, eating ice cream, writing postcards and taking holiday photos.

Suddenly something strange happened. 'The sea began to bubble first. Then it was gone! All the water rushed out and where we were standing, there was no water any more!' Tilly said. Her parents and many other people wanted to follow the water.

Tilly was scared. For a moment, she closed her eyes. She saw herself at school, in a Geography lesson in October or November. 'I heard my teacher,' Tilly said, 'Mr Kearney, talking to us about the dangers of tsunamis. "Before there is a tsunami," I heard Mr Kearney's voice, "the water goes back. Then people have five or ten minutes to run quickly out of the water. When the water comes back, it comes back very, very fast and high and it's really dangerous."

'Mummy, we must get off the beach now! I think there's going to be a tsunami!' Tilly shouted. At first, her parents didn't understand. 'Mum! Dad! A big wave! It's dangerous! Let's run!' Tilly shouted. When people heard that, they started to shout, 'Off the beach. Run! A dangerous wave is coming!' Tilly and her parents ran away from the beach. They ran back to the hotel and went up to higher floors. All the other people ran away from the beach too. They followed Tilly and her family.

Then the water came back. It was very high and fast and there was a lot of noise. The water broke trees, huts and small houses. In many parts of Thailand and other countries, the tsunami killed lots of people.

On Maikhao Beach all the people were safe. They were safe because ten-year-old Tilly Smith remembered her Geography lesson. And they were safe because Tilly reacted so quickly when she saw what was happening.

 **Think!** **Work in pairs. How many different endings can you find for these sentences?**

1 Tilly was happy in Thailand because …

2 Tilly was on the beach. She looked around and saw …

3 When Tilly saw that the water rushed out, she …

4 The other people …

5 Tilly saved many lives because …

Work in pairs. Choose a role: the reporter or Tilly. Plan and act out an interview.

| Where were you … ? | Who did you go with? | What were you doing when … ? | How did you know … ? | What did you do? | Where did you go when the big wave … ? |

FIRE SAFETY

1 **What should you do? Read and tick (✓) the correct picture.**

In case of fire in the house

1. Never hide in your wardrobe or under beds. You need to leave the room.
2. Leave the house quickly, but don't run.
3. Close doors behind you.
4. Don't look for things to take with you.
5. When there is smoke, crawl on the floor. The air is safest near the floor.
6. Ring the emergency services.

1

2

3

4

5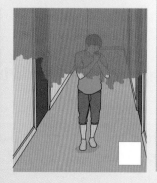

6

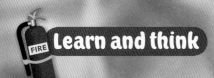

① **Think!** **Look at the school plan. Draw the safest escape route.**

You are in ...	The fire is in ...	Draw the safest route in ...
classroom 5	the toilets	green
the library	the staff room	blue
classroom 2	classroom 6	orange

② **Project** **Work in groups. Make an escape plan for your school.**

1 Make a floor plan of your school. 2 Draw in escape routes.

3 Have a practice fire drill. 4 Write a report of the fire drill.

On Wednesday we did a practice fire drill. It worked well.
We got to our meeting place in two minutes, but there were
some problems. Two students tried to take their bags.
One boy lost a shoe. When he picked it up, a girl fell over him.

Act out

Emergency!

1 Choose a role card. Read and plan.

STUDENT A

Imagine there is an emergency situation. You want to call the emergency services. Before you do so, think about the following:

- What is the emergency?
- Where are you?
- Who needs help?
- Who is with you?

STUDENT B

Imagine you work for the emergency services.

- Find out what the problem is.
- Ask where the caller is.
- Find out who needs help.
- Find out who the caller is with.

Useful language

Emergency services	Caller
Hello, this is … How can we help you?	I'm calling because there is a fire (an accident, a flood, …)
Where are you calling from?	I'm in … (Street), opposite / near / in front of the …
Who needs help?	A child / man / woman. He / She can't … He/She is in pain …
Who is with you?	I'm on my own. / There is a …
Are you safe?	Yes, I am. / No, I'm not because …
OK. Don't worry. The police / an ambulance / a fire engine / will be there in …	Thanks very much.

2 Act out your play.

Emergency services. How can we help you?

Hello, this is … speaking. I'm calling because …

my scrapbook

Story telling

1. **Read Amy's stories about the same accident. <u>Underline</u> the words and sentences in Text B that are not in Text A. Which text is better? Why?**

A

It was last May.
We were on our
bikes. One of my
friends, Adrian,
took a bottle of
water out of his
rucksack and
started to drink.
He fell.
Amy

B

It was a beautiful day last May. 'Let's ride our bikes!' my friends shouted. 'Great!' I said. We had lots of fun! It was sunny and warm. Then one of my friends, Adrian, took a bottle of water out of his rucksack and started to drink. Suddenly he fell. 'Ouch!' he shouted. There was blood on his knees. Poor Adrian!
Amy

2. **Read Joel's story. Make it more interesting.**

It was last weekend. My mum and I wanted to visit my grandparents.
We were in the car. We saw an accident. Mum phoned the ambulance.
Mum phoned the police. They came ten minutes later.
Joel

3. **Now write a story about an accident. It can be a true story or you can imagine it.**

1. Use some of the <u>underlined</u> words and sentences from Activity 1 and from your version of Joel's story to make it interesting.

2. Draw a picture.

- When did it happen?
- What happened?
- Who were you with?
- Who was hurt?
- What were you doing?

4 Two return tickets

Listen and say the words. Then check with a friend.

1. station
2. platform
3. escalator
4. ticket office
5. train driver
6. stairs
7. rucksack
8. suitcase
9. a cup of coffee
10. a cup of tea

LONDON £21
CAMBRIDGE £18
OXFORD £12
HULL £38
BLACKHILL £14
BEDFORD £27
BRISTOL £28
NEWCASTLE £42

WOODBRIDGE

Tickets

PLATFORM
1

CAFÉ

CD2 17 **Listen and answer.**

1 Where do Ben and Lucy decide to go?
2 How much are the tickets?
3 When does their train leave?
4 What do they do before they leave?

Play the prices game.

Two return tickets to London, please.

OK.

How much is it?

That's £42.

1 CD2 18 **Match the questions with the answers. Listen and check.**

1 When does the train leave?

2 When are you going to eat next?

3 When's your birthday?

4 When did you get this watch?

5 When are you going to give me my present?

6 When are we going to play football?

a In the afternoon. We're going to meet in the park at three.

b I'm not sure. In 2011, I think.

c At dinnertime.

d On your birthday.

e At eight o'clock from platform 2.

f It's in May.

2 CD2 19 (Grammar focus) **Listen and say.**

My birthday is **in** September.
The train leaves **at** eight o'clock.
Let's have the party **on** Sunday.
My grandparents visited us **in** the morning.
I like reading outside **in** summer.

3 **Play the true or false game.**

1	My birthday is in December.
2	This year it's on a Sunday.
3	I always watch TV at seven o'clock.

Number 2 is false.

That's right.

CD2 20 Listen and complete the song.

Mr Knocks, Mr Knocks.
He's got five big orange clocks.
Tick tock, tick tock,
Tick tock, tick tock.

(1) _____ Monday (2) _____ three,
He always climbs the apple tree.
(3) _____ Tuesday (4) _____ six,
He always goes and buys some bricks.
(5) _____ Wednesday (6) _____ two,
He always sails his red canoe.
(7) _____ Thursday (8) _____ four,
He always paints his garage door.
(9) _____ Friday (10) _____ five,
He always goes out for a drive.
(11) _____ Saturday and Sunday,
He only sits and waits for Monday.

Tick, tock ...

Mr Knocks, Mr Knocks
With his five big orange clocks.
But (12) _____ a Monday (13) _____ June,
He flew off up to the moon!

Now poor old Mr Knocks
Hasn't got his orange clocks.
Mr Knocks, Mr Knocks
Hasn't got any orange clocks! Oh no!

It's two o'clock.

CD2 21 Listen and sing.

Play the miming game.

1 Read and tick (✓) the correct sentences.

1   When the train arrived, a man was reading a paper.

2   Two girls with rucksacks were waiting on the platform.

3   A man was cleaning the windows of the ticket office.

4   Two dogs were playing with a ball.

5   A boy was eating a pizza and two men were eating hot dogs.

  Listen and say.

> I **was having** dinner when you **phoned** me.
> When I **arrived** at the party, my friends **were dancing**.
> A boy **was eating** an ice cream when the train **arrived**.
> When the train **arrived**, two men **were eating** hot dogs.

  Work with a friend. Think of sentences.

1   When I came home from school, our dog …

2   My dad … when I came into the living room.

3   When my parents came home, my big brother and I …

4   When I came into the garden, my friends …

5   My teacher … when I arrived at school.

6   When I started my homework, my sister …

The tunnel

1

Lucy: I'm still thinking of your grandpa's story. When is he going to tell us?
Ben: I don't know, but I hope it's good!
Lucy: Our train is coming now. Quiet, Buster!

2

Ben: What stop is this?
Lucy: Let's see. It's Broom. … Oh no! Horax and Zelda! I hope they can't see us.
Ben: Get away from the window!

3

Horax: Ha! You can't escape! Where's the map?
Lucy: We haven't got it here.
Horax: Open your rucksacks.

4

Horax: Zelda, check the book. Maybe they put the map in there.
Ben: Look! We're going into a tunnel. Now's our chance!

5

Ben: Buster, good dog. Say hello!
Horax: Yuck! Get down! Stop that dog! Zelda, stand near the door! Those kids mustn't escape!

6

Conductor: Tickets, please … thank you.
Horax: Hey, our tickets! I put them in my hat.
Zelda: Oh no! Our tickets disappeared when we were going through the tunnel.

Conductor: You must get off the train at the next station.
Horax: But I had the tickets.
Conductor: Here's the station now. Off you go.

Lucy: That trick of yours was great. Look at Horax and Zelda. They don't look very happy!
Ben: Lucy, look over there! I don't believe it. It's the line: 'Climb more stairs and look out west'.

2 **Think!** **Put the story in order.**

☐ Horax and Zelda have to get off the train.

☐ In the tunnel Ben takes Horax and Zelda's tickets.

☐ Ben sees the line of the rhyme.

☐ At Broom station Lucy sees Horax and Zelda.

☐ Lucy and Ben get on the train.

☐ The conductor wants to see the tickets.

☐ Horax looks for the map in Ben's rucksack.

☐ Horax can't find their tickets.

3 **Find the stairs and the pear in the story.**

4 **CD2 25** **Listen and say.**

Bears on stairs, bears on chairs, hairy bears are everywhere!

1 Look at the pictures and read the story. Write some words to complete the sentences about the story. You can use 1, 2 or 3 words.

Last weekend Jim, his mum and his dad wanted to go to a museum in another town. On Saturday morning Jim woke up late, so they had to hurry to the train station. At the station Jim saw a cap in a shop window. He wanted to have it. He asked his dad, but his dad first said no. 'Dad, please, this cap looks so cool. I haven't got a cap and it's hot and sunny today. Can I have it?' Finally his dad said yes. Now Jim was hungry and thirsty and wanted to go to a restaurant, but at that moment their train arrived and they got on it.

At the next station a woman got on and sat down opposite Jim and his parents. Jim was very hungry now. After half an hour the train stopped. 'There was an accident with a car,' the conductor said. 'We have to wait for the emergency services.' The woman opened her bag and took out a sandwich and an apple. Jim looked at her. When she looked up, he quickly looked away. The woman smiled and asked Jim's parents, 'Can I give him something to eat?' 'That's kind,' they answered. The woman put her hand in her bag and gave Jim a sandwich and an orange. Jim thanked her. He was very happy.

1   Jim and _____ wanted to go to a museum.

2   Jim's dad first didn't want _____ a cap for Jim.

3   The train arrived so they couldn't _____ restaurant.

4   The train stopped _____ there was an accident.

5   The woman could see that Jim _____ .

6   She _____ a sandwich and an orange.

Skills

CD2 29

Listen and tick (✓) the correct time.

1

A ☐ B ☐ C ☐

2

A ☐ B ☐ C ☐

3

A ☐ B ☐ C ☐

4

A ☐ B ☐ C ☐

5

A ☐ B ☐ C ☐

6

A ☐ B ☐ C ☐

Work in pairs. Look at the pictures. Make sentences.

1  2  3  4

5  6  7  8

9  10

When I went into the park, …

… a boy was drinking water.

Learn and think

FORCES

1 Read and circle.

1   A push is a force **away from / towards** the centre of the force.

2   A pull is a force **away from / towards** the centre of the force.

Pushes and pulls are forces. Forces make things move.

Push

Pull

2 Look at the pictures. Which show a 'push'? Which show a 'pull'?

3 Read and write the name of the force in the picture.

Forces around us

Why does an apple fall to the ground when it drops from a tree? Why don't people float about in the air? The answer to both these questions is a very important force. It's called gravity. Gravity pulls objects towards Earth. Without it, we would all fly off into space.

1 Read and write *rough* and *smooth* under the pictures.

When you go down a slide, gravity pulls you to the bottom, but there is also a force trying to stop you. It is called friction.

If a surface is smooth, like a slide, the friction is smaller. You go faster.

If a surface is rough, the friction is bigger. You go more slowly.

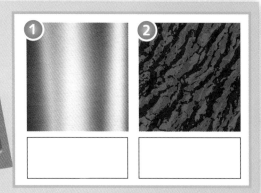

2 Project Do experiments to measure friction.

1 Take a book and cover it with foil. Put an object at one end.

2 Slowly lift up the end of the book with the object on it.

3 When the object starts sliding, stop lifting. Measure the height of the book above the desk.

4 Repeat the experiment, covering the book in a towel and then in sandpaper.

3  What do you notice? Read and circle.

On a smooth surface, the object starts sliding **earlier / later**.
On a rough surface, the object starts sliding **earlier / later**.

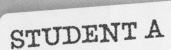

Act out

At the train station

1 Choose a role card. Read and plan.

STUDENT A

You want to go on a train trip. At the ticket office you tell the person where you want to go. You ask about:

- the price of a single ticket
- the price of a return ticket
- the time when the next train leaves
- the platform number
- the time when it arrives

STUDENT B

You work at the ticket office. You tell the tourist:

- the price of a single ticket
- the price of a return ticket
- the time when the next train leaves
- the platform number
- the time when it arrives

Useful language

Tourist	Ticket office assistant
I want to go to …	
How much is a single ticket?	A single ticket is …
How much is a return ticket?	A return ticket is …
When does the train leave?	At …
When does it arrive?	At …
What platform number is it?	Platform …
Thank you very much.	You're welcome.

2 Act out your play.

Thank you very much.

my scrapbook

A school notice

4

1 Read this notice from a school board. Tick (✓) the checklist and <u>underline</u> the information.

School trip

We're going to visit Brighton on 2nd September.

Travel by train.

Meet outside the station at 8.30 a.m.

£7.50 per person (return).

The return train arrives at 5.30 p.m.

Checklist

Information to put in a notice about a school trip:
- where you're going to go ☐
- date ☐
- meeting point ☐
- meeting time ☐
- cost ☐
- return time ☐

2  Read these three notices. What information is missing from each one? Use the checklist to help you.

School trip

Join our trip.

Meet in front of the school. Bring warm clothes and good shoes.

Cost per person £12.50.

Return to school at 4.30.

Join us!

We're organising a trip to the Blue Lake. Meet at the bus stop in Green Lane at 9 o'clock on 5th October. Return to school at 5 o'clock.

We're going to visit London on 15th November.

Meet on platform 2 at the train station at 8 o'clock.

Price per person £9.

3 Write a notice for your school board. Use the checklist to help you.

5 Police!

CD 2 31 **Listen and say the words. Then check with a friend.**

1. dark
2. blonde
3. fair
4. moustache
5. curly
6. beard
7. scar
8. straight

CD 2 32 **Listen and correct the sentences.**

1. Grandpa was a teacher.
2. He chased a criminal for 30 years.
3. The criminal was very stupid.
4. Grandpa knows the criminal's name.

Play the describing game.

She's got short hair. It's curly and it's dark.

It's Ana.

58 Hair and face

1 Look, read and number the sentences.

a   Many years ago Ben's grandpa used to be a police officer. ☐

b   He used to drive a fast car. ☐

c   He used to carry a walkie-talkie. ☐

d   He used to chase dangerous criminals. ☐

e   He used to catch dangerous criminals. ☐

f   Now he isn't a police officer. His life is much quieter. ☐

2 CD2 33 Grammar focus Listen and say.

He **used to be** a police officer. (But he isn't now.)
He **used to work** all night. (But he doesn't now.)
He **used to wear** a uniform. (But he doesn't now.)

3 Are any of these sentences true for you? Tick (✓) them. Write two more.

1   I used to walk to school with Mum but now I walk with my friends. ☐

2   I used to have curly hair but now it's straight. ☐

3   I used to watch cartoons on TV but now I watch sport. ☐

4   I used to have one brother but now I've got two. ☐

5   I used to have a teddy bear but I haven't got one now. ☐

6   I used to like milk but I don't like it now. ☐

1 CD2 34 **Listen to the song. Draw how Dad's hair used to be.**

Dad before

Dad now

Dad: I used to have some curly hair.
It was long and I dyed it fair.
I went down to the hairdresser's
And now there's nothing there.

Son: Who are you?
Dad: Take a look.
I'm your dad.
Son: No, you are NOT!

Dad: I used to have a big moustache,
Thick and dark – like a real rock star.
And then I tried to cut it off
And now there's just a scar.
Who are you?

Dad: I used to have a long black beard,
But now it's in the bin.
I shaved it off the other day
And now there's just my chin.
Who are you?

2 CD2 35 **Listen and sing.**

3 Think! **Look at the pictures. How are the people different now?**

Aunt Mary | Uncle John | Cousin Dave

before   after   before   after   before   after

Aunt Mary used to have …

1 CD2 37 **Listen, read and circle.**

1 Grandpa had to be careful because
**there were lots of dangerous criminals /
he had a dangerous dog.**

2 He didn't tell his wife anything because
**he had to keep things secret /
she wasn't interested.**

3 He had to wash his uniform every **week / day.**

4 Ben can't be a police officer because
his clothes are often dirty / he's too small.

2 CD2 38  **Listen and say.**

We **had to be** really careful.
We **had to keep** everything secret.
We **had to wear** a uniform.
We **had to wash** our uniform every week.

3 **Look at the pictures. Ben's grandpa went to police camp for six months.
What did he have to do?**

He had to do the washing up.

The Mysterious H

1

Grandpa: The Mysterious H started robbing jewellers. He used to steal necklaces, bracelets and watches. There wasn't a shop in London which was safe.

2

Grandpa: His next plans were cleverer. He stole famous paintings and works of art from museums all over the world.

3

Grandpa: Then he stole the Queen's crown. The story was in all the papers. I had to find this man quickly.

4

Grandpa: He went to Paris and stole the top of the Eiffel Tower too!
Lucy: What!

5

You look here.
You look there.
But you can't find
me anywhere.

Ben: But Grandpa, how did you know it was the same man?
Grandpa: He used to leave us a note. It always had the same symbol on it – the letter *H*.

6

Lucy: Did you catch him?
Grandpa: No. We almost caught him once, but he escaped.

7

Ben: It's a great story, but I don't understand. What's the connection with the waiter at the restaurant?

8

Grandpa: Ah, the waiter was wearing a ring with the letter *H* … the same *H* that was on the notes … that The Mysterious H used to leave.
Ben and Lucy: Wow!

2 **Write *t* (true) or *f* (false).**

1 The Mysterious H robbed jewellers all over London. ☐

2 He only robbed places in England. ☐

3 He stole the Queen's ring. ☐

4 The Mysterious H went to Paris. ☐

5 He always left the police a note. ☐

6 The waiter in the restaurant had an *M* on his ring. ☐

3 **Find the car and the horse in the story.**

4 **Listen and say.**

Martha the farmer's doing art – drawing on her horse and cart!

1 Look at the pictures. Find someone who looks:

happy   scared   sad   angry

2 CD2 43 Read and listen. Check your answers.

Yatin and the orange tree

Yatin Indra sat under the orange tree with his grandson. He stood up and picked an orange from the tree. He cut it into two pieces and gave half of it to his grandson to eat. He watched the little boy eat the fruit and smiled. 'Did I ever tell you my story about this tree?' Yatin asked. 'No,' his grandson said. 'Well, let me tell you,' and Yatin began his story.

'It was a hot sunny day. I was a little boy like you and I sat under an orange tree to keep cool from the sun. I looked up and saw a big juicy orange. I knew it was wrong because it wasn't our tree, but I was so thirsty. I picked the fruit and ate it. It was delicious. I looked back at the tree and picked another.'

'Then I felt a big hand on my shoulder. I looked around and saw the most frightening man in the village. It was Gautam Kahn, the meanest farmer and enemy of all the children. "I'm sorry," I said. "It's just one orange," but Kahn didn't want to listen. He told me to wait and left his dog to watch me. "Let's see what the police officer has to say," he said. "You stay here. I'm going to get him."

'I didn't know what to do. The police officer was coming. I was in trouble. I couldn't go anywhere, not with that dog there. I thought about my parents. They would be angry. I thought about the oranges. It was bad to take them. I knew it was wrong but they were so delicious.'

'Then Gautam Kahn returned. He had the police officer with him. "This is the boy," he said and pointed at me. "He stole my oranges." "Is it true?" the police officer asked. "Yes, it is," I said. "I know it was wrong," I added, "but it is so hot and the oranges were so juicy." The police officer looked at Gautam Kahn. "Do you really want me to take this boy to the police station?" he asked. "The boy is sorry."

Gautam Kahn looked at me. He wasn't so angry. "Well," he said, "the boy could work for me for the rest of the day."

"What do you think?" the police officer asked me. "Yes," I said, "of course."

'I worked all day for Gautam Kahn. I was tired but I wasn't sad. At the end of the day, the farmer came to me. He was happy now. "Thank you," he said. Then he gave me a little bag. "In this bag there are some orange tree seeds," he said. "Plant them and you will never again have to take fruit from other people's trees." Then he told me to go home.'

Yatin Indra looked at his grandson. His story was finished. He pointed up at the orange tree behind them. 'And this, my dear, is the tree which grew out of my seeds. Every time I eat an orange from it, I think about Gautam Kahn and the lesson that I learnt.'

3 Answer the questions.

1 Why did the young boy Yatin take an orange?

2 Why was Yatin scared of Gautam Kahn?

3 Where did Gautam Kahn go?

4 Why couldn't Yatin run away?

5 What did Gautam Kahn give Yatin?

6 What does Yatin think when he looks at the tree?

4 Complete the story.

Yatin took an (1) _____ from a (2) _____ . The (3) _____ caught him.
The farmer went to get the (4) _____ . He left his (5) _____ to watch
Yatin. The (6) _____ didn't want to take Yatin to the (7) _____ .
Then the (8) _____ asked Yatin to (9) _____ for him.
Yatin worked hard. The (10) _____ gave Yatin a bag of (11) _____
to say thank you. Yatin grew his own (12) _____ .

CRIME FICTION

1 **Think!** **Read and decide which of these people are real.**

Agatha Christie (1890–1976) was an English crime writer. In her most famous books, the reader must guess who did the crime and why. Her novels are still popular all over the world. In the 1930s she was in a real life mystery when she disappeared for 10 days. Nobody knows where she went.

Sir Arthur Conan Doyle (1859–1930) was a Scottish writer. He created the world's most famous detective, Sherlock Holmes. He was one of the first people to make crime novels very popular. Many people say that he is the father of crime fiction. He also wrote science fiction and historical novels.

Jane Marple is one of Agatha Christie's most famous detectives. She is an elderly woman who never married. She enjoys watching people and sees everything. She always finds the murderer. She first appeared in 1930 in *Murder at the Vicarage* and then appeared in 11 more novels.

Sherlock Holmes is a detective who Conan Doyle created. Holmes is famous because he always thinks a lot to solve crimes. His friend Dr Watson usually helps him. Holmes often has his best ideas when he is relaxing and playing the violin.

Hercule Poirot is another of Agatha Christie's detectives, famous for his moustache! He is from Belgium and solves crimes all over Europe. He first appeared in 1920 and then appeared in 32 more novels and 51 short stories.

2 **Work in groups. Ask and answer.**

1 Do you know these TV and film detectives?
2 What other famous detectives on TV or in films do you know?
3 Do you like crime stories? Why (not)?

> I like crime stories because they are exciting.

> I don't like crime stories because they are boring.

Learn and think

1 CD2 44 **Listen, read and match.**

Murder on the Orient Express

Hercule Poirot is travelling on the Orient Express. On his second night on the train, he wakes up because there are strange noises. The next morning someone finds a dead body in the compartment next to his. Poirot investigates and finds out that the dead man was also a murderer. Poirot also thinks that other people on the train are happy because the man is dead. But who killed him and has Poirot got enough time to solve the murder before the train arrives?

Detective	Place	Crime	Suspects

Murder   People on the train   Hercule Poirot   Train

2   Project **Plan a crime story.**

1 Copy and complete the table with notes for your own crime story.

Detective	Inspector Thinly
Place	A hotel in Scotland
Crime	Murder of a man
Suspect	The woman in room 12A

2 Write a summary.

> Inspector Thinly is from Scotland. This story takes place in a hotel. A cook finds a dead man in the garden. One of the people in the hotel heard a shout in the night. It came from room 12A. The woman in 12A is missing in the morning ...

Reading habits

1 **Ask questions and write names.**

David, do you read more than one book a week?

No, I don't.

Elena, do you read in bed?

Yes, I do.

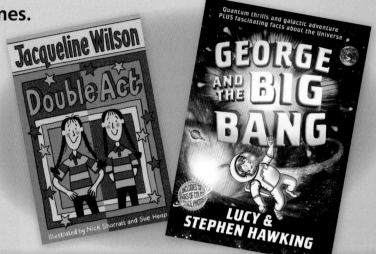

Name:	This person ...
Pedro	reads more than one book a week.
Elena	reads in bed.
	likes adventure stories.
	likes funny stories.
	reads comics.
	doesn't like crime stories.
	's parents have got books in other languages at home.
	doesn't use a library outside school.
	hasn't got a book of poems.
	prefers reading to computer games.

2 **Work in groups. Talk about what you found out.**

Toni reads in bed.

Luca likes funny stories.

A book review

1 Read the two book reviews. Which one is better? Why?

a

Book review
'A true friend' by RJ Glass.
This book is about Erin.
She hasn't got any friends.
Then she gets some
friends. I liked this book.

b

Book review
'A true friend' by RJ Glass.
This book is about a girl called Erin. Erin
hasn't got many friends because she is shy.
One day a new student arrives at Erin's
school and her life is never the same again.
I liked this book because it was very exciting.

2 Use the notes to write a review.

Book:	The Clown
Author:	Robert Wise
Main character:	Jim / popular / very funny
What happens?	forgets how to laugh / loses his friends
What did I think?	good / funny

3 Think of a book and make notes.

4 Write a review. Draw the cover.

Book:

Author:

Main character:

What happens?

What did I think?

6 Mythical beasts

CD3 02 Listen and say the words. Then check with a friend.

1 tail
2 horn
3 back
4 scales
5 wing
6 neck
7 feathers
8 tongue

CD3 03 Listen and answer.

1 How did Ben know about the dragon?
2 What is Ben holding?
3 Why is this the right place?
4 Where do they look last?

Think! Play the animal game.

I'm thinking of an animal. Can you guess?

Has it got wings?   Can it ... ?

CD3 04 **Read and write *t* (true) or *f* (false). Then listen and check.**

Dino facts – or dino myths?

1   The biggest dinosaur was longer than ten cars.   ☐
2   The fastest dinosaurs could run at 60 km/h.   ☐
3   T-rex was one of the most dangerous dinosaurs.   ☐
4   The heaviest dinosaur was more than 80,000 kilos.   ☐
5   The best dinosaur film is called *Planet of Dinosaurs*.   ☐
6   The worst dinosaur film is called *Legend of the Dinosaurs*.   ☐

CD3 05 **Listen and say.**

The **biggest** dinosaur was **longer than** 10 cars.
The **heaviest** dinosaur was more than 80,000 kilos.
Meat-eaters were **more dangerous than** plant-eaters.
T-rex was one of **the most dangerous** dinosaurs.
This book is good but there's a **better** dinosaur book in the library.
Is *Jurassic Park* **the best** dinosaur film of all time?
The special effects are **worse** in old dinosaur films.
Which is **the worst** dinosaur film?

3  **Work in groups. Write six sentences for an animal quiz.**

A correct sentence = 1 point

Only **your** group writes this sentence = 3 points

African elephants are *bigger than* Indian elephants.	True / False
Cats are *friendlier than* dogs.	True / False

Listen to the song. Read and circle.

Last night I had the strangest dream.
I went back millions of years and saw
Amazing things on planet Earth
And I met the most beautiful dinosaur.

Its head was (1) **big / bigger** than a tractor.
Its neck was (2) **shorter/ longer** than a tree.
Its scales were (3) **strong / stronger** than stone
And its tail was (4) **big / bigger** than me.

It said, 'Climb on my back.'
I did and then we flew up high.
I saw the moon, the sun and stars
On my dino in the sky.
Last night ...

It had the (5) **strongest / longest** wings on Earth.
This dinosaur was (6) **faster / slower** than light!
It took just half an hour for us
To fly around the world that night!
Last night ...

It was scaly and scary but beautiful too!
The most beautiful, beautiful, beautiful dinosaur!

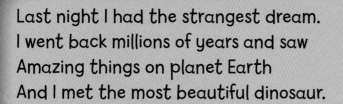

 Listen and sing.

 **Write sentences for a friend to read.**

THEDINOSAURINMYDREAMWASBIGGERTHANMYHOUSE

MYDINOSAURWASTHEFASTESTANIMALINTHEWORLD

1 **CD3 08** Look at the beasts. Write the names under the pictures. Listen and check.

Pegasus   the Sphinx   a mermaid   a unicorn   the Phoenix   a centaur

Did you know?

Around the world there are lots of stories about mythical beasts. These beasts often look like animals, but sometimes they are half animal and half human.

2 **CD3 09** **Grammar focus** Listen and say.

What **does** a unicorn **look like**?
It **looks like** a white horse, but it's got a big horn.
What **does** a centaur **look like**?
It's half horse and half human.

3 Take it in turns to close your book. Ask and answer.

MULTICORN

MINISAURUS

MERDOG

PHOEFISH

What does the multicorn look like?   It looks like Pegasus, but it has got …

The secret door

1

Lucy: Ben, come over here.
Ben: What is it?

2

Lucy: Look. There's a little door. Let's open it.
Ben: Good idea. Let's see what's inside.

3

Ben: I hope it's not a trap!
Lucy: Me too! Now, let's start looking for that line.

4

Horax: Now we've got you! (*He laughs.*) Give us the map or you have to stay in there forever!

5

Ben: We can't get out of that door. What can we do?
Lucy: Hmm, look! There's a ladder. Maybe it's a way out. It's our best chance!

6

Lucy: We can get out here. Let's jump into the pool, but be careful with the map!
Ben: It's in my jacket. I just hope that Horax and Zelda aren't looking.

7

LOOK DOWN AND FIND THE TREASURE CHEST

Lucy: They're still there! But they can't see us.
Ben: Hey, look here – on the side of the pool!
Lucy: It's the next line: 'Look down and find the treasure chest'. Great! Now let's go. Hurry up!

8

Ben: Lucy, run!
Zelda: Oh no, look!
Horax: Stop, you two! We're going to get you!

2 Read and make sentences.

1 Lucy finds
2 They leave the door open
3 When Horax closes the door,
4 Lucy has an idea how
5 Horax and Zelda
6 The map doesn't get wet

a when they go down the stairs.
b because it's in Ben's jacket.
c shut the door.
d a way into the dragon.
e he is sure he is going to get the map.
f to get out of the dragon.

3 Find the feathers on the beast in the story.

4 CD3 11 Listen and say.

King Dean's got gold beans, but Heather's treasure is feathers.

Skills

CD3 14 **Listen and tick (✓) the box.**

1 Where did Paul find the book?

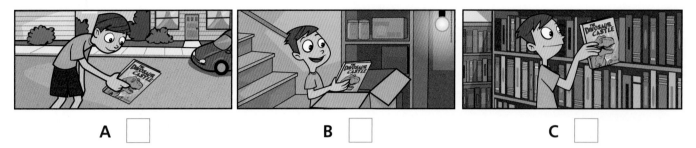

A ☐   B ☐   C ☐

2 Where did the dinosaurs in the book live?

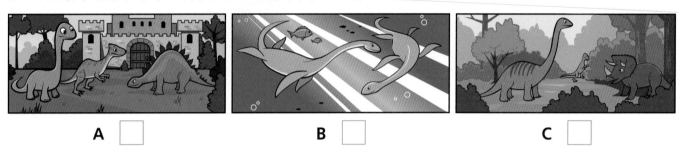

A ☐   B ☐   C ☐

3 What did they eat?

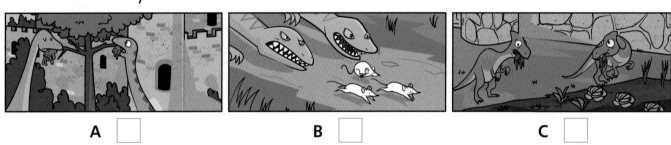

A ☐   B ☐   C ☐

4 What happened to the book?

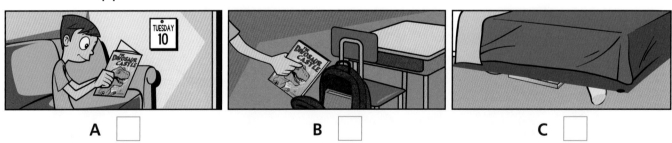

A ☐   B ☐   C ☐

5 What did Paul give his sister?

A ☐   B ☐   C ☐

 **Skills**

1 **Work in pairs. Make a list of words for each picture.**

2 **Tell the story with a friend.**

One day Shelly and her friends were in the park. They ...

3 **Now write the story.**

One day Shelly and her friends were ...
Shelly ...   She ...
In the morning ...
It had ...
A week later ...

Protection

① **Think!** Read and look at the photo. Which animal is the predator? Which is the prey?

All animals must eat. Animals which eat other animals are called *predators*. They are always looking for their next meal. Their *prey* (the animals which they like to eat) must try not to be that next meal. Animals have different tricks to survive. These tricks are very important.

② **How do prey animals protect themselves against predators? Read and match the titles with the text.**

Poison   Looks   Weapons   Speed

1 _____

You are an **antelope** and you see a big cat watching you through the grass. What do you do? Run! Speed is the simplest way and one that is used by many animals, fish and birds. Prey animals that are faster than their predators have a good chance of escaping. They can't eat prey that they can't catch!

2 _____

Look closely at the pattern on the wings of this **moth**. What do you see? Many predators look and see two big eyes. They are scared of the animal. They think it is a much bigger animal, so they go away and look for something smaller.

3 _____

Some animals have weapons that make them very difficult to eat. Look at this **porcupine**, for example. The spikes are very hard and can hurt a predator.

4 _____

Other animals produce chemicals from their body. This **dart frog**, for example, has got poison in its skin. The bright colours tell the predators, 'I'm poisonous. You mustn't eat me.'

1 **Think!** How do these animals protect themselves?

rabbit   turtle   butterfly   skunk

2 Think of more predators and their prey. How do the prey animals protect themselves? Discuss with a friend.

Owls and eagles are the predators of snakes.

Many snakes are poisonous.

3 **Project** Find out about an animal.

1 Work in groups. Choose an animal from your country.

2 Find a photo or draw a picture of it.

3 Find out:
- Where does it live?
- What does it eat?
- What are its predators/prey?
- How does it protect itself?

4 Present your animal to the class.

Our animal is …

It lives …   It eats …   Its predators …   It can …

4 Write five true / false questions about your animal to test the class.

OUR HEDGEHOG QUIZ

1 Hedgehogs have weapons.   True / False
2 Hedgehogs are poisonous.   True / False
3 Hedgehogs can run fast.   True / False
4 Mice are the predators of hedgehogs.   True / False
5 Worms are the prey of hedgehogs.   True / False

Act out

Finding an unusual animal

1 Choose a role card. Read and plan.

STUDENT A

You are in the park and you see a very unusual animal. Think about the following:

• What does it look like?
• Has it got wings (fur / claws ...)?
• Can it swim (fly / run very fast ...)?

Now phone the zoo. Tell the director about the animal and ask what you should do.

STUDENT B

You are the zoo director. Someone is going to phone you to tell you about an unusual animal. Think about what you want to know:

• Looks?
• What can it do?

Make a decision about what to do.

Useful language

Finder

Hello, am I talking to the director of the zoo?
I've got a strange animal.
It looks like ...
It's got ...
It can ...
It's faster than / bigger than / smaller than ...

Director

What exactly does it look like?
What colour is it?
Has it got ... ?
How big ... ?

2 Act out your play.

What exactly does it look like?

It's got a long body ...

My beast

1 **Read Ryan's text. Add eight full stops.**

• full stop

This was the unicornix It lived a million years ago and it was the heaviest animal in those days It was pink and it looked like a horse It had a big horn on its head It also had wings with lots of beautiful feathers They were green and gold The unicornix could fly and it was faster than the fastest bird It could also swim and run and it was one of the most dangerous animals in the world

2 **Read the text aloud to check. Pause after each full stop.**

3 **Read Tammy's text. Add capital letters and seven full stops.**

the minirex was the smallest dinosaur in the world it was smaller than a mouse it was half dinosaur and half bird and it also looked like a fish it had horns and wings the wings had feathers its tail was long and full of scales it was the fastest animal under water

4 **Imagine and draw a mythical beast. Write about it.**

- What was its name?
- When did it live?
- What did it look like? (Another animal? Did it have horns / wings / feathers / a tail / scales … ?)

- Was it heavier or smaller than other animals? Was it the biggest, the fastest … ?
- What could it do? (Fly? Swim? Run very fast … ?)

7 Orchestra practice

CD3 16 Listen and say the words. Then check with a friend.

1. tambourine
2. triangle
3. trumpet
4. trombone
5. drums
6. harp
7. saxophone
8. keyboard
9. violin

CD3 17 Listen and correct the sentences.

1. Lucy and Ben arrive last.
2. Ben knows other musical places.
3. They check six instruments.
4. They can look again at lunchtime.

Play the miming game. Ask and answer.

Are you playing the violin?   Yes, I am.

CD3 19 **Listen and write the names.**

Theo   Jade   Rosy   Tom   Hannah

 CD3 20 Grammar focus **Listen and say.**

It's **my** guitar. = It's **mine.**   It's **your** guitar. = It's **yours.**
It's **his** guitar. = It's **his.**   It's **her** guitar. = It's **hers.**
It's **our** guitar. = It's **ours.**   It's **their** guitar. = It's **theirs.**

Play the *Whose is it?* game.

Is this yours?

Yes, it's mine. Thank you.

1 CD3 21 **Listen and complete the song.**

Children: Today there's chaos in the classroom.
No-one can find their stuff.
There's chaos in the classroom.

Teacher: Let's tidy up. Enough's enough!

Children: Whose is this pen, the silver pen?
Hey, Sandra, is it (1) _____ ?

Sandra: Let's see. It really isn't (2) _____ .
Ask Sue, I think it's (3) _____ .

Today there's chaos ...

Children: Tim and Nick, look over there.
Are those green rulers (4) _____ ?

Tim and Nick: Oh no, they aren't – (5) _____ are blue!

Teacher: So tell me, whose are they?

Today there's chaos ...

2 CD3 22 **Listen and sing.**

3 **Write and sing your own verse.**

Whose is this car, the orange car?
Hey, Horax, is it yours?
Let's see. It really isn't mine.
Ask Zelda, I think it's hers.

Listen and match the children with the instruments and the houses.

Vicky   Christina   Claire   Connor   Josh   Mark

  Grammar focus **Listen and say.**

Connor's the boy **who** plays the recorder.
The instrument **which** Vicky plays is the trumpet.
The house **where** Mark lives is green.

Look at the pictures. Follow the lines and make sentences.

Shona   Harry   Liam   Anna   James   Katy

The instrument which Shona plays is …   The house where …

who / which / where 85

At the concert hall

1

Conductor: OK, time for a break. You can all go to the café now and have a drink and a snack.
Ben: Shall we stay here and look for the line?

2

Lucy: Let's go for a drink first. I'm thirsty.
Ben: I'm hungry too. We can look later.
Lucy: Good idea.

3

Ben: Orange juice and an apple, please.
Lucy: And hot chocolate and a banana for me, please.
Assistant: Here you are.

4

Ben: Hey, I can see something which you can't … the line! It's on your cup!
Lucy: Is it? Well spotted! What does it say?
Ben: 'In the lighthouse you will see.'

5

Horax: Ha! Here's the map which is going to make me rich and famous. I knew it! Very nice of you, kids. Thank you.

6

Conductor: What are you doing in here? It's the junior orchestra. You shouldn't be here.
Horax: Erm … I'm sorry, I'm so sorry.
Conductor: Leave now! Before I call the police.

7

Lucy: Oh no! Look! Your rucksack's open.
Ben: The map! Where is it? Horax! He was *here*!
Lucy: Oh no! We can't do anything now.
We have to play.

8

Lucy: Hey, there's the map!
Ben: Cool!

  Cover the story. Complete the sentences.

1   Lucy and Ben play in …
2   Lucy plays … and Ben plays …
3   During the break they …
4   In the café they find …
5   When they come back, they …
6   The map …

 Find the girl with short curly hair in the orchestra.

 Listen and say.

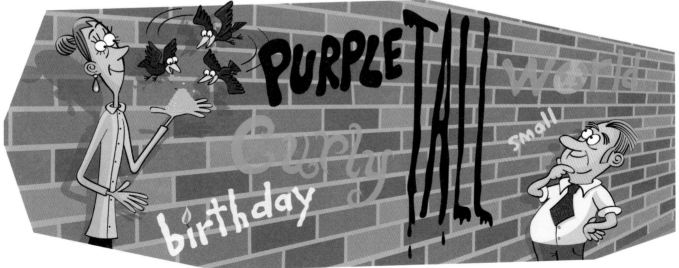

Fern is tall. She's feeding birds. Bert is short. He's reading words.

Story time

  Listen. Which animal is it?

| bear | wolf | woodpecker | deer | boar |

Read and listen.

The bear's dream

The bear was a friendly animal and had many friends.
In the morning, the bear and his friends used to play games
by the river and in the evening, they used to sit in the sunset.
The bear loved listening to his friends' stories. He could also
tell very good stories himself.

One day, when the bear was walking down to the river, he
saw a car. It was going very fast and suddenly a big bag fell off the car roof. The driver didn't stop.
The bear looked into the bag and it made him very happy. In the bag there was the most beautiful
violin in the whole wide world.

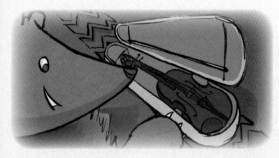

From that moment on, the bear had a dream. He wanted
to be a violin player. He played his violin in the morning,
he played it at lunchtime and he played it in the evening.
At night, when he was tired from all the playing, he
dreamt of his violin. He dreamt that he was a violin player
and, in his favourite dream, he dreamt that he was giving
a concert to a big group of friends.

One day, the bear went to see his friends. 'I am
now a violin player,' he said, 'and I'd like to invite
you to my concert on Sunday at seven o'clock by
the river.' His friends thanked him.

When it was Sunday, everybody was excited.
The bear waited for his friends to sit down. Then
he closed his eyes and he started to play. He played
for two hours and he didn't stop for one minute.

88 Value: enjoying being different; reading skills

When he finished, he turned and he looked at his friends and waited.

His friends were silent. They didn't shout 'Hooray!' They didn't clap their hands and they didn't say a word. They were silent for a long time. Then the wolf began to speak. 'Dear bear!' she said. 'We love you very much, but you're a bear and **not** a violin player!' The animals laughed and a minute later they all left.

The bear was now alone. He looked at the sun. The sun was going down. The bear started to think. 'I think the wolf is wrong!' he thought. 'I **am** a violin player!'

The bear didn't forget his friends. He still played with them and went to their parties, but the bear didn't invite his friends to hear him play the violin any more. He played his violin every day for many hours. He played it in the morning, he played it at lunchtime and he played it in the evening. He played and played and played and played because he loved it ... and the forest birds loved it too.

 **Answer the questions.**

1 Why did the bear have a lot of friends? _____

2 How did the bear find the violin? _____

3 Why did the bear play the violin all the time? _____

4 What did the bear want most? _____

5 Did his friends like his music? _____

6 Was the bear sad about what the wolf said? _____

Think! **Imagine you are the bear. How do you feel when the wolf talks to you after the concert?**

I feel ...

I want to ...

I love ...

How we make sounds

1 CD3 31 **Listen to these sounds. Answer the questions.**

1 Which sound is louder: 1 or 2?

2 Which sound is higher: 3 or 4?

2 CD3 32 **Listen again and number the photos.**

3 **Look at the photos in Activity 2. Answer the questions.**

1 In which photo is the rubber band shorter?

2 In which photo is the rubber band longer?

3 In which photo is the bang on the drum louder?

Learn and think

7

1 **Think!** Look and think. Make true sentences with *louder*, *quieter*, *higher* and *lower*.

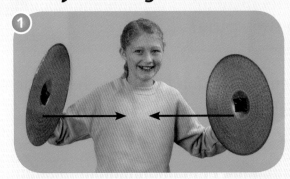

The girl's cymbals are going to make a …

2 **Project** Work in pairs or groups. Make a wind chime.

1 Make an X with two rulers or sticks and tie them together.

2 Tie short lengths of string onto metal spoons of different lengths.

3 Tie the strings onto the rulers.

4 Blow to make the wind chime sound.

Find out

Music in our class

1 Work in groups. How many students play an instrument? What instruments do they play?

Students who play an instrument	Students who don't play an instrument	Instruments
✓✓✓	✓✓✓✓	recorder ✓✓
		guitar ✓

2 Ask the students who don't play an instrument: Would you like to play an instrument? Which one?

Would like to play an instrument ✓✓	Wouldn't like to play an instrument ✓✓
drums ✓	
saxophone ✓	

3 Find out about your class.

- favourite singer
- favourite band
- favourite song
- a song you really don't like

4 Write the results on the board. Then write a report.

Music in our class

In our class there are 19 children: 11 girls and 8 boys. 12 play a musical instrument. 8 children play the recorder, 2 play the guitar, 1 plays the drums and 1 plays the keyboard. Our favourite singer is Justin Bieber. 10 children like him. Our favourite band are JLS. We all think they're great. A song we really don't like is 'Only girl in the world' by Rihanna. We think it's awful! Only Chloe likes Rihanna!

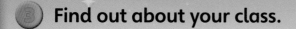

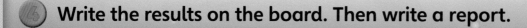

My music review

my scrapbook

1. **Read Shannan's text. Look at the words in colour. Write the short forms.**

I love music. My favourite (1) singer is Laura Gold.
(2) She is 24 years old and (3) she is an excellent singer.
My favourite Laura Gold (4) song is 'Goodbye'. I often
listen to it before I fall asleep. (5) She has also got a
song called 'Paper flowers'. (6) It is fantastic. Now
(7) Laura has got a new song, 'Sweet dreams'. (8) I do not
think (9) it is very good because she sings without a band.

(1) _____
(2) _____
(3) _____
(4) _____
(5) _____
(6) _____
(7) _____
(8) _____
(9) _____

2. **Write Tyler's text again. Use short forms.**

I have not got a favourite singer,
but I have got a favourite band.
They are called 4by4. Nick is the
drummer. Sharon and Rick play the
guitar. Keith plays the trumpet. Their
most successful song is 'Dancing
in the sunset'. I love it because the
words are really cool. The music is
good too. My sister has got all their
songs on MP3.

3. **Think of your favourite band or singer. Write a text using short forms. Add photos or drawings.**

- name
- favourite song(s)
- why you like him / her / them
- why you like it / them

8 **In the planetarium**

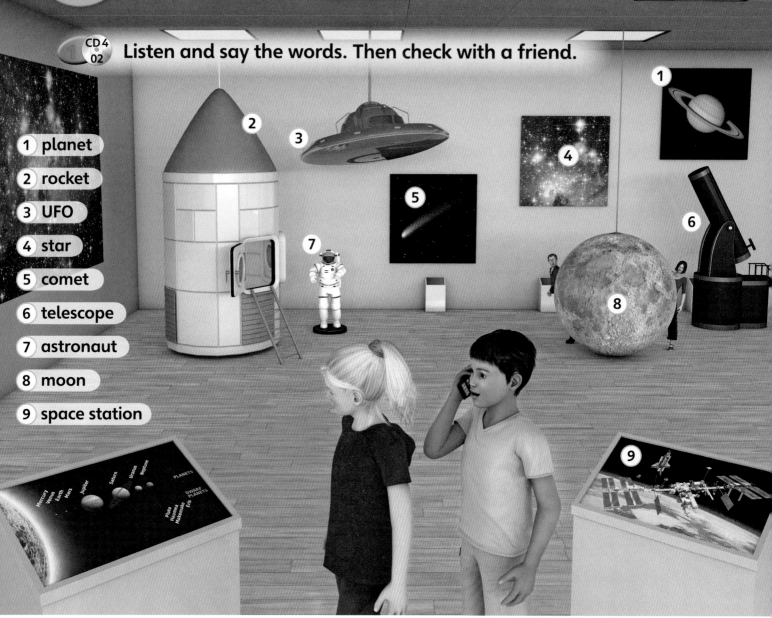

CD4 02 **Listen and say the words. Then check with a friend.**

1 planet
2 rocket
3 UFO
4 star
5 comet
6 telescope
7 astronaut
8 moon
9 space station

CD4 03 **Listen and answer.**

1 Who is Ben calling?
2 Is Grandpa at the planetarium?
3 What question does Ben answer?
4 Where is the telescope?

Describe and guess.

It's something which you use to look at the stars.

A telescope!

It's someone who …

CD4 04 **Make sentences. Listen and check.**
What do you think? What will you be when you grow up?

1 I'll be a teacher …

2 I'll be a photographer …

3 I'll be an astronaut …

4 I'll be an ambulance driver …

5 I'll be a police officer …

a and I'll catch dangerous criminals.
b and I'll work with children like me!
c and I'll take pictures of lots of different cities.

d and I'll go really fast.
e and I'll visit the moon.

CD4 05 **Grammar focus** **Listen and say.**

What **will** you **be** when you grow up?
I'll be an astronaut and **I'll visit** the moon.

Ask and answer.

What will you be when you grow up?

I'll be a zoo keeper. I'll look after the lions.

1 CD 4 06 **Listen to the song and number the pictures.**

One day I'll be an astronaut
And I'll fly through space.
I'll live in a space station
In a far away place.

I'll climb inside a rocket
And fly up to the moon.
I'll whizz about in outer space
And not come back too soon.
One day ...

I'll ride on a comet
And hold on to its tail.
I'll whizz about in outer space
And look back at our trail.
One day ...

I'll meet some friendly aliens
On Jupiter and Mars.
I'll whizz about in outer space
And visit all the stars.
One day ...
... In a far away place.

2 CD 4 07 **Listen and sing.**

3 **Imagine you are an astronaut. What will you do?** I'll meet ...

1 Look, read and number the sentences.

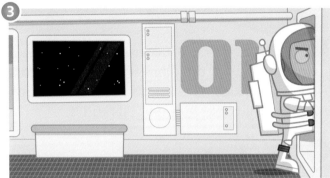

a   The astronaut put on his spacesuit carefully. ☐

b   He opened the space station door slowly. ☐

c   He stepped through the door quietly. ☐

d   Whoops! Wrong door! ☐

 CD 4 08 **Grammar focus** **Listen and say.**

He hurt his head **badly**.	We did our homework **carefully**.
She left the house **quickly**.	They walked home **slowly**.

3 Give a friend instructions with adverbs.

Put your book on your head carefully.

Walk to the door slowly.

Sing a song quietly.

Touch your nose quickly three times.

1

Lucy: I can't see a line anywhere.
Ben: No. I don't think it's here. Let's go for a drink and we can think about it.
Lucy: Good idea.

2

Horax: 'Look at the planets, look at the stars.' Ha! Stupid kids. The line will be on this map!
Zelda: Ah! Look! A poem! I'll read it.

3

Off to the moon we go for a ride.
Go over there and climb inside.
There you'll find the final line.
Find my treasure with this rhyme.

Zelda: 'Off to the moon we go for a ride.
Go over there and climb inside.
There you'll find the final line.
Find my treasure with this rhyme.'

4

Horax: That's easy. It's inside the rocket! Come on! Let's look carefully.
Zelda: The treasure is almost ours!

5

Horax: Hey, what's happening? ... Oh, those kids!
Lucy: It was a trick. We knew you were here!
Ben: And I knew you were listening to my phone call. There *isn't* a planet on the map.

6

Lucy: And there *isn't* a line here. We wrote the note and the poem to trick you!
Horax: Let us out!
Ben: I can't. But here's someone who can.

Ben: Grandpa! Your plan worked perfectly.
Grandpa: I knew it! My friend is going to take Horax and Zelda to the police station. He's got a lot of questions for them.

Ben: Now we can find the last line with no more trouble.
Grandpa: And maybe I will find the answer to a mystery of my own.

2 Answer the questions.

1 Did Ben and Lucy know that Horax and Zelda were there?

2 Where does Zelda find a poem?

3 Who wrote the poem?

4 What do Horax and Zelda want to find in the rocket?

5 What are the police going to do at the police station?

6 What is Grandpa's mystery? What do you think?

3 Find the *ladder* in the story.

CD4 10 **Listen and say.**

A surf*er* saves a snake charm*er*, a danc*er* and a farm*er*!

 Skills

1 CD 4 13 **Listen, colour and write.**

2 **Look at the picture in Activity 1 and read. Write *yes* or *no*.**

1 There are three windows in the rocket.

2 The aliens have got three eyes.

3 The astronaut is scared.

4 It is raining and the aliens are holding an umbrella.

5 The astronaut has got a flag in both hands.

6 The astronaut is shaking hands with the fattest alien.

1 **Think!** Talk about the pictures. Find the odd one out.

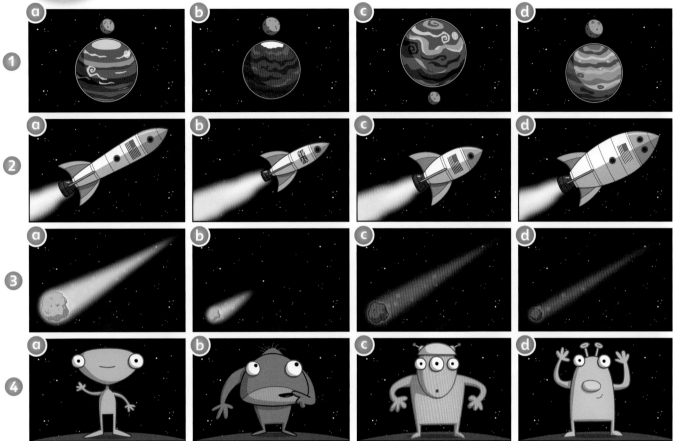

2 **Read Leo's postcard. Then complete his parents' conversation.**

Dear Mum and Dad,
I'm having a wonderful time here on the moon. The journey here was quite long. It was about two days but I slept most of the way. I like the space station. It's really big and there's lots to do. The only thing which isn't very good is the food.
I'll be home in a month.

Lots of love,
Leo

Mum:	We've got a postcard from Leo!
Dad:	(1) _____ ?
Mum:	On the moon. Don't you remember?
Dad:	Oh yes! (2) _____ ?
Mum:	About two days.
Dad:	(3) _____ ?
Mum:	Yes, he does. It's big and there's lots to do.
Dad:	(4) _____ ?
Mum:	No, it isn't. It isn't very good at all!
Dad:	(5) _____ ?
Mum:	In a month.

3 **Imagine you're on the moon. Write a postcard to your parents.**

The Solar System

1 CD4 14 **Listen and point to the planets.**

These are the planets in our solar system. They all orbit our sun.

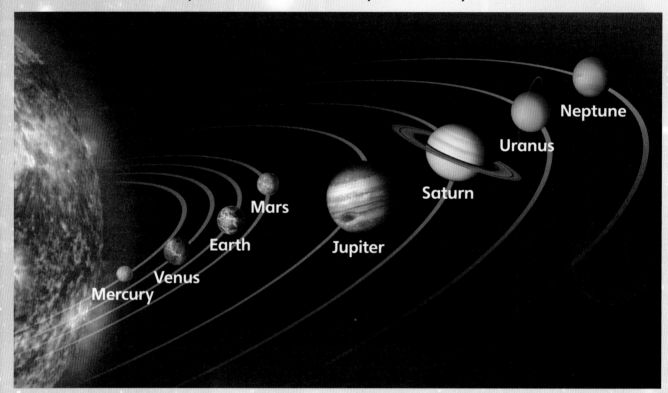

Neptune

Uranus

Saturn

Mars

Earth

Jupiter

Venus

Mercury

2 **Read the text. What is the sun?**

Our solar system has 8 planets. The word *solar* means 'of the sun' and at the centre of our solar system is the sun. All the planets go around the sun. We say they *orbit* the sun. Each time a planet makes one orbit of the sun, it completes a year, but these 'years' are not all the same as ours. Planets that are not far from the sun have shorter years; planets that are further from the sun have longer years. On Earth, a year is 365 days, but the planet that is furthest from the sun takes 60,000 Earth days to orbit it (about 165 Earth years).

The sun is not a planet. It is a star. It is the only star which we can see in the daytime. The sun's diameter (the distance from one side to the other side through the centre) is more than 1,000,000 kilometres! The sun is so big that you could put a million Earths inside it.

Many of the planets have a moon. This is a smaller object that orbits a planet. Earth has 1 moon but some planets have more than 50.

① **Think!** **Look at the table. Then read and write *t* (true) or *f* (false).**

	Diameter (km)	Day temperature (°C)	Distance from the sun (million km)	Length of year (Earth days)
Mercury	4,880	350	58	88
Venus	12,104	480	108	225
Earth	12,756	22	150	365
Mars	6,792	−55	228	687
Jupiter	142,984	−123	778	4,332
Saturn	120,536	−180	1,429	10,750
Uranus	51,118	−214	2,875	30,707
Neptune	49,532	−220	4,504	60,202

1 Saturn is the biggest planet in our solar system. ☐
2 Neptune is further from the sun than Mars. ☐
3 Mercury has the shortest year. ☐
4 Jupiter is the furthest planet from the sun. ☐
5 Venus is the hottest planet in our solar system. ☐
6 Earth is further from Mars than it is from Venus. ☐

② **Write four sentences to test a friend.**

③ **Project** **Find out about moons in our solar system.**

1 Work in groups. Use the Internet or a library to find out:
 • Which planets in the solar system have got one or more moons?
 • Which planets in the solar system haven't got any moons?
 • Interesting information about the moon(s), e.g. name(s), size(s), etc.

2 Write a report.

This is what we have found out about moons in the solar system.
... planets have no moon at all.
The planet with the most moons is ...   It has got ...
There are ... with one moon.

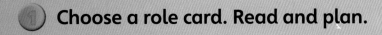

Act out

Interview an alien

1 Choose a role card. Read and plan.

STUDENT A

You are an astronaut. You are going to talk to an alien on the planet Og. Think of questions to ask:

- his / her name and age
- what he / she does
- his / her family
- what Og is like
- other things which you want to know (How … ? Why … ?)

Ask and answer questions.

STUDENT B

You are an alien who lives on planet Og. You are going to talk to an astronaut from Earth. Think about:

- your name and age
- what you do
- your family
- what Og is like
- other things which you want to tell the astronaut

Ask and answer questions.

WELCOME TO OG

Useful language

Astronaut	Alien
Is this Og?	Yes, it is. Welcome to my planet!
What do you do … ?	I'm a …
Can you tell me about your family?	Yes, I've got …
What is Og like?	It's very …
How (do you travel on Og)?	We (have flying cars).
Why (have you got three heads)?	Because (we use …)

2 Act out your play.

Why have you got three heads?

Because …

A diary entry

1 **Read the space diary entry. Number the pictures in order.**

Friday, 12th March

Today we landed on the moon. First we looked carefully out of the window. There were no monsters waiting for us. Then we put on our spacesuits. After that we opened the door of the spaceship. Finally we walked down the ladder to the moon.

2 **Complete this diary entry with the red words from Activity 1.**

Wednesday, 7th June

Today we went on a long trip. (1) _____ we flew quickly from Planet XR3 into outer space. It was a fantastic journey and we saw a beautiful comet. (2) _____ we explored the centre of a very big solar system called Galaxy 17. There we met with our friends from Jupiter. (3) _____ we went round Galaxy 17. (4) _____ we returned to Earth. Where will we go tomorrow?

3 **Copy and complete the notes about Thursday. Use your own ideas.**

flew to explored met	I saw: a new solar system, lots of

4 **Write Thursday's diary entry. Use the red words from Activity 1.**

9 At the campsite

CD 4 / 16 **Listen and say the words. Then check with a friend.**

1. sail a boat
2. swing on a rope
3. dive into the water
4. row a boat
5. dry your clothes
6. make a raft
7. put up a tent
8. make a fire
9. collect wood

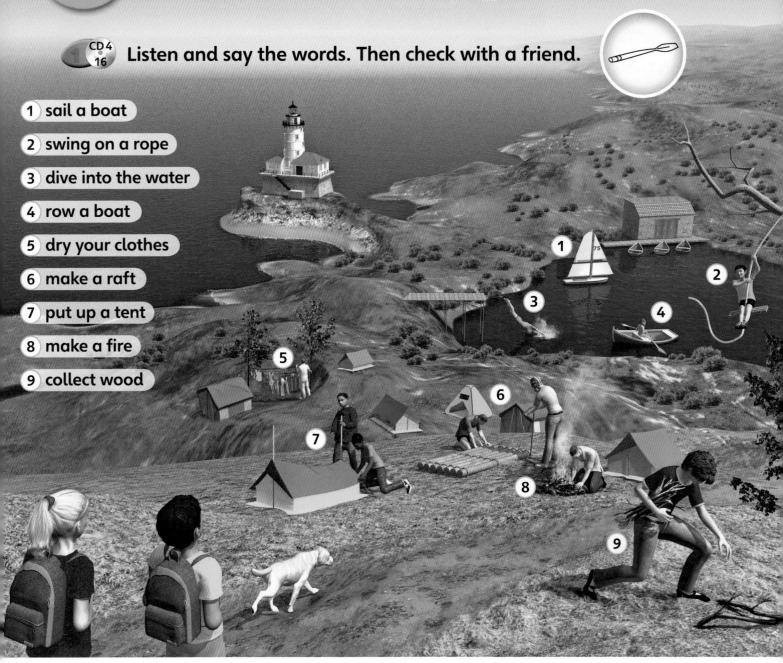

CD 4 / 17 **Listen and correct the sentences.**

1. Lucy wants to make a fire.
2. They are going to sail a boat.
3. Horax and Zelda are there.
4. Zelda is the Mysterious H.

Play the drawing game.

What was I doing at 5 o'clock?

Were you putting up a tent?

9

CD 4 18 Look, read and number the sentences. Listen and check.

a Let's get some cheese. ☐

b There's some water in that glass. ☐

c We must get some bread. ☐

d There's a loaf of bread on the table. ☐

e Let's get some lemonade. ☐

f Can I have this can of lemonade, please? ☐

g That's a big piece of cheese! ☐

h Can you get three bottles of water, please? ☐

i Open that packet of crisps carefully, please. ☐

j Let's buy some crisps for the party. ☐

CD 4 19 Grammar focus Listen and say.

Here's **a loaf of** bread.

Let's buy **a big loaf of** bread or maybe two **loaves**.

Let's buy **some** tomatoes.

A can of tomatoes, please.

Here's **a bottle of** milk.

Let's buy **a packet of** sweets.

Let's get **some** cheese.

That's **a big piece of** cheese.

Work in groups. Organise a picnic.

Let's get some crisps.

OK, I can bring three packets.

We need …

1 CD 4 20 **Listen to the song. Circle the food.**

We're going on a picnic
With our picnic basket.
Mum put a piece of cheese
In our picnic basket.

We're going on a picnic
With our picnic basket.
Mum put a loaf of bread
And a piece of cheese
In our picnic basket.

We're going on a picnic
With our picnic basket.
Mum put a bottle of juice,
A loaf of bread
And a piece of cheese
In our picnic basket.

We're going on a picnic
With our picnic basket.
Mum put a packet of crisps,
A bottle of juice, a loaf of bread
And a piece of cheese
In our picnic basket.

We're going on a picnic
With our picnic basket.
Mum put a bar of chocolate,
A packet of crisps, a bottle of juice,
A loaf of bread and a piece of cheese
In our picnic basket.

And so we ate and ate and ate and ate
And ate and ate until ...

We ate all the picnic
In our picnic basket.
We had a bar of chocolate,
A packet of crisps,
A bottle of juice, a loaf of bread
And a piece of cheese, so there's
Nothing in our basket! Oh!

2 CD 4 21 **Listen and sing.**

3 **Draw a picture. Play the picnic basket game.**

Is there a piece of cheese
in your picnic basket?

No, there isn't.

Are there any bottles
of lemonade?

Yes, there are
two bottles.

1 CD 4 22 **Listen, find and write numbers in the table.**

2 CD 4 23 Grammar focus **Listen and say.**

How many bottles of water do we need?
How much cheese do we need?
How much bread do we need?
How much bars of chocolate do we need?

3 **Take it in turns to close your book. Play the memory game.**

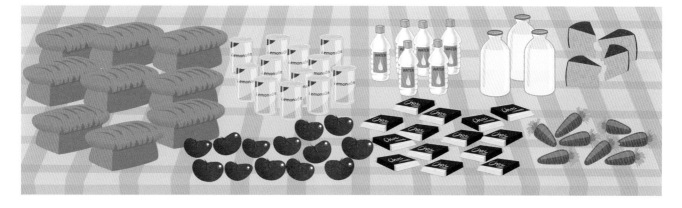

How much bread is there?

I think there are nine loaves.

How many carrots are there?

I think there are …

How much? / How many? **109**

CD4
24

The last line

1

Lucy: We'd like to hire a rowing boat, please.
Assistant: How long do you want it for?
Ben: An hour, please.
Assistant: OK, that's £5.

2

Ben: Oh, where's the line? I'm getting very tired.
Lucy: Hey, look – on the oar! It's the last line!
Ben: You're right. 'There's the key to end this game.' Great, we've got all six lines!

3

Ben: OK, let's put the rhyme in order. I think this is the first line: 'In the lighthouse you will see'.
Lucy: And there's a lighthouse on the beach near the campsite! Come on!

4

Ben: Well, this is stair 33.
Lucy: And there's the picture.
Ben: I'm getting very excited.
Lucy: Me too.

5

Ben: Look, the key! Now we have to find the chest which this key opens.
Lucy: We have to climb more stairs first. I think we have to go to the top.

6

Ben: 'Climb more stairs and look out west.'
Lucy: Which way is that?
Ben: The sun sets in the west. It's over there.
Lucy: And look at the floor down here!

Lucy: That's it, Buster! Find the chest!
Ben: Here's the key. Look, it fits!
Lucy: Wow! This treasure is beautiful!
Ben: And now we can take it to the museum.

Horax: Why did I wear that ring? How stupid!
Zelda: No, it's the children who are stupid.
They gave that treasure to the museum.
Horax: Again? Oh no!

② Answer the questions.

1 For how long do Ben and Lucy hire a boat?
2 Where do they find the last line?
3 Where is the lighthouse?
4 Where do they find the key?
5 How does Ben know which way is west?
6 What does Zelda think of the children?

③ Find *a cup of tea* in the story.

④ CD4 25 Listen and say.

*A **piece** of **cake**, a **cup** of **tea**. **On** the **lake** – **just you** and **me**.*

  Read the story quickly and try to find the answers.

1 What are the names of the children?

2 Where are the children going?

3 They find an animal. What is it?

 CD4 28 **Read and listen. Check your answers.**

The snares in the forest

'What are we going to do tomorrow?' asked Jane. 'The weather isn't good enough to swim.'
  'We could sail a boat or make a raft,' said Tom. Jane didn't like those ideas. 'It'll rain and then we'll need to dry our clothes.' 'What about going into the forest?' suggested Jack. 'Great idea,' said Sue, 'maybe we'll find some mushrooms.'
  'Do you know which mushrooms are safe to eat?' asked Jane. 'Yes, I do. I used to pick mushrooms with my grandma,' said Sue, 'and we can cook them over the fire in the evening.' The next morning, Jane, Sue, Jack and Tom walked up the hill behind the campsite and into the forest.

They didn't find any mushrooms, but they found a snare. In it there was a young rabbit. The snare was around one of its legs. The children carefully removed the snare and picked up the rabbit. Luckily it wasn't hurt and it ran away. 'Snares are bad,' said Sue angrily. The children looked around and found two more of them.

They took sticks and poked the two snares until they pulled tight. Then they put the snares safely in their rucksacks. 'Don't forget the one which caught the rabbit,' Jane said. 'No, let's leave that one here,' Jack answered, 'because I've got an idea.'
  'What's that?' asked Jane. 'I'll tell you later,' said Jack. 'Let's go back to the campsite and have our dinner.'

After dinner Jack told the others his plan. Before it got dark, the four children walked up the hill and into the forest again. They arrived at the place where they found the little rabbit and put an old hat into the snare. Then they tied white T-shirts onto sticks and hid behind some trees. They waited until it was dark. After half an hour they heard two people talking.

The voices were coming closer very quickly. Then they saw two of the oldest boys from the camp. 'It's here,' said one of them. 'Look, there's a rabbit in the snare,' the other boy said. 'Let's take it, set the snare and go back. I don't like it when the forest is so dark.' The boy went to pick up the snare. At that moment, Jack shone the torch at the T-shirts. The others made horrible noises. 'Ghosts!' one boy shouted. 'Let's run!' The two boys ran away as fast as they could. Jack, Jane, Tom and Sue looked at each other and laughed. 'Those two boys won't set snares any more,' Jack said.

3 Read and make sentences.

1 Tom wanted to make
2 The next morning the children
3 They wanted to
4 They found a
5 The children took
6 Later they went back into
7 They also tied
8 They scared the older boys

a find some mushrooms.
b two snares and left one.
c the forest and hid.
d who came to find their snare.
e a raft.
f white T-shirts to sticks.
g small rabbit in a snare.
h walked into the forest.

4 Look at the pictures. Use the words to tell the story.

forest mushroom snare rabbit plan rucksack T-shirt stick ghost scare

1

2

3

4

5

Map reading

CD 4 30 **Look, listen and point to the symbols on the map.**

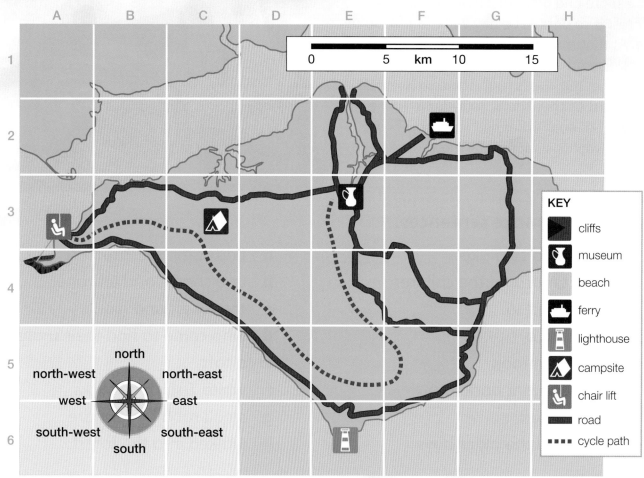

KEY

▶ cliffs
🏺 museum
⬜ beach
🚢 ferry
🗼 lighthouse
⛺ campsite
🚡 chair lift
— road
•••• cycle path

north
north-west   north-east
west —— east
south-west   south-east
south

2 **Work with a friend.** ⟨ Point to the north-west. ⟩

3 Think! **Read and find on the map.**

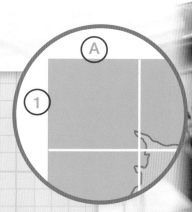

Grid references

A **grid reference** on this map has a letter and a number.
The grid reference for the campsite is C3.

Look at the map. Tick (✓) or correct the grid references.

1 lighthouse E6 _____   2 museum G3 _____

3 ferry A3 _____   4 cliffs A4 _____

① Think! **Read and measure on the map on page 114.**

Scale

We use the **scale** of a map to find out about distance. The scale of this map is 2 cm = 5 km. This means that 2 centimetres on the map is the same as 5 kilometres on the ground.

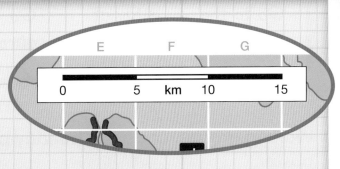

Are these distances correct? Tick (✓) or cross (✗).

1 To get from the beach to the lighthouse, you have to drive more than 15 km. ☐

2 To get from the museum to the ferry, you have to drive about 3 km. ☐

3 To get from the chair lift to the campsite, you have to cycle about 10 km. ☐

4 The cycle path is longer than 90 km. ☐

② Think! **What scale would you use for these maps?**

1 a map of your classroom

2 a map of your school

3 a map of your village, town or city

4 a map of your country

③ Project **Work with a friend. Make a map of your neighbourhood.**

1 Write a list of what you want to include on your map.

2 Create your own symbols and a key.

3 Guess the distances between these things in real life.

4 Decide on a scale. Draw the outline of your map with grid references.

5 Add the symbols from your key.

④ Present your map to the class.

This is a map of …

The scale is: 1 centimetre equals …

On our map you can see …

Find out

Holiday plans

1 Make a class list of holiday plans on the board.

Go to the beach	Stay at home	Go abroad	Do a holiday club	Go camping
✓✓✓✓	✓✓✓✓✓	✓	✓✓	✓✓✓✓

2 Work in groups. Choose a holiday plan. Ask and answer. Make a poster.

> What are you going to do on the beach?

> I'm going to read lots of books.

3 Tell the class about your poster.

> Four children are going to go to the beach. Bruno is going to learn to surf.

> Paulo is going to read lots of books on the beach.

> Ana is going to fly her kite.

> Lucía is going to eat lots of ice cream and build a big sandcastle.

A holiday leaflet

1 Read the leaflet. What do you like about this campsite?

Come to Haverigg Campsite!

Where is it?

This beautiful campsite is near the beach. You can come by train from Barrow (45 minutes) or by bus from Millom (5 minutes).

What can you do here?

You can learn to surf and sail a boat here because there is a water sports centre.

Where can you visit?

There's a lake near the campsite where you can see lots of different birds. The lighthouse in Haverigg is very old, so it's a fascinating place to visit.

2 Plan a leaflet for a campsite or holiday camp.

1 Fold a piece of paper for your leaflet.
2 Choose a real or imaginary place.
3 Find or draw pictures of the correct size.
4 Write texts in pencil on small pieces of paper.
5 Arrange your pictures and texts.

3 Check your text.

1 Does your leaflet give useful information?
2 Are there any interesting adjectives?
3 Can you make longer sentences with:
   - *and, because, so* or *but*?
   - *who, which* or *where*?

4 Make your leaflet.

What has the campsite got?

Haverigg Campsite

We have got everything! This campsite has got shops and a café (with Internet).

Prices:
Small tent £30 (1 night), £50 (weekend), £120 (a week)
Big tent £45 (1 night), £75 (weekend), £150 (a week)

Well done, Ben and Lucy!

Simple present questions

Do you **speak** English?	Yes, I **do**.	**Are** you happy?	Yes, I **am**.
Does John **like** pizza?	No, he **doesn't**.	**Is** it cold?	No, it **isn't**.
Do they **go** to your school?	Yes, they **do**.		
When **do** you **have** Maths?	How **does** he **spell** his name?		
What's your favourite number?	What time **do** you **have** lunch?		

1 **Complete the sentences.**

1 _____ you tired?

2 _____ she like dogs?

3 What time _____ you get up?

4 _____ your dad drive you to school?

5 _____ your English homework difficult?

Simple past questions

Did he **enjoy** the film?	No, he **didn't**.	When **did** he **see** it?	On Monday.
Were you at school on Friday?	Yes, I **was**.	**Was** it nice?	Yes, it **was**.

1 **Make questions.**

1 they / did / win / match / the / ?

_____

2 interesting / was / lesson / the / ?

_____

3 you / your / do / did / homework / ?

_____

4 did / that / you / buy / jumper / where / ?

_____

1 In the museum

Must / Mustn't

I **must go** to bed early tonight.
He **must be** more careful.
Dogs **must be** on a lead.

You **mustn't tell** anyone.
She **must be** there by nine o'clock.
We **mustn't make** a noise.

1 Write *must* or *mustn't*.

1 I _____ tidy my room today.

2 They _____ do their homework tonight.

3 We _____ show this to anyone. It's a secret.

4 You _____ be quiet. Your little sister's sleeping.

5 We _____ talk in class. Our teacher gets angry.

Direct and indirect objects

I sang **my baby brother a song.**
Don't ask **them the same question!**

Don't tell **him the secret!**
Give **it a bath**, please.

1 Make sentences.

1 his / give / Rex / ball

_____

2 show / your / me / picture

_____

3 this / made / Dad / skateboard / me

_____

4 take / some / flowers / Grandma / let's

_____

5 stories / them / Grandpa / great / tells

_____

② The world around us

Simple past revision; connectors

They went to the park **and** they played football.
I was late **because** the bus didn't come.
He didn't study, **so** he didn't pass the test.
I went fishing, **but** I didn't catch anything.

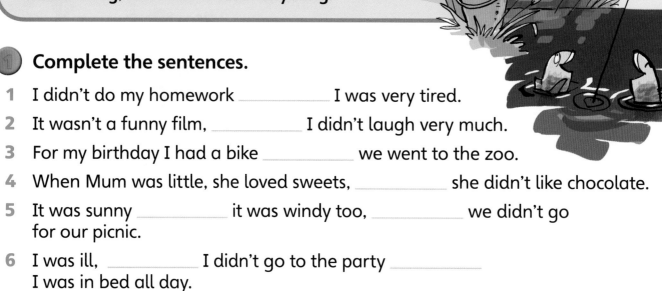

1 Complete the sentences.

1   I didn't do my homework _____ I was very tired.

2   It wasn't a funny film, _____ I didn't laugh very much.

3   For my birthday I had a bike _____ we went to the zoo.

4   When Mum was little, she loved sweets, _____ she didn't like chocolate.

5   It was sunny _____ it was windy too, _____ we didn't go
    for our picnic.

6   I was ill, _____ I didn't go to the party _____
    I was in bed all day.

Could / Couldn't

I **couldn't speak** English when we first moved to the UK.
She **could play** the piano when she was three!
Could you **talk** when you were one?   No, I **couldn't**.
Could they **dance** when they were younger?   Yes, they **could**.

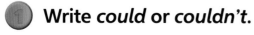

1 Write *could* or *couldn't*.

1   I _____ phone you because I was busy.

2   It was dark, so she _____ see anything.

3   We _____ speak Italian because we lived in Rome.

4   Dad _____ lift me up high when I was little. He can't now!

5   Mum _____ run very fast and she won all the school races.

③ Danger!

Past continuous

> At two o'clock in the park …
> I **was playing** with my friends.
> Mum **was reading** a newspaper.
> My friends **were running**.
>
> You **were sleeping**.
> We **were having** a lot of fun.
> The cat **was eating** the picnic.

1 Complete the sentences.

It was six o'clock.

1 I _____ playing the guitar.
2 My sister _____ watching TV.
3 The dog _____ chasing the cat.
4 Mum and Dad _____ working in the garden.

Past continuous questions

> Yesterday evening …
> What **were** you **doing**?
> What **was** he **doing**?
> **Was** Mum **working**?
> **Were** they **having** fun?
>
> I **was helping** my dad.
> He **was doing** the washing up.
> No, she **wasn't**.   **Were** you **reading**?   Yes, I **was**.
> Yes, they **were**.   **Was** it **raining**?   Yes, it **was**.

1 Complete the sentences.

Think about yesterday afternoon.

1 _____ you watching TV?   Yes, I _____ .
2 _____ Dad playing the piano?   No, he _____ .
3 _____ your brothers swimming?   Yes, they _____ .
4 What _____ Mum doing?   She _____ reading.
5 What _____ you doing?   I told you! I _____ watching TV!

4 Two return tickets

at / in / on

School starts **at** nine o'clock.
My sister's birthday is **in** January.
Mrs York came to this school **in** 2011.
I have swimming lessons **at** four o'clock **on** Wednesday afternoons.

I can't sleep **at** night when it's very hot.
It's very hot **in** summer.
What was he doing **in** the morning?

1 Complete the sentences.

1 Mum met Dad _____ 1995.
2 The film starts _____ seven o'clock.
3 We went shopping _____ the afternoon.
4 I don't like playing outside _____ winter.
5 We're going to fly to Canada _____ Monday.

Past continuous and simple past

When the phone **rang**, I **was brushing** my teeth.
They **were playing** football when the storm **started**.
The cat **was chasing** a mouse when it **hit** its head.

1 Read and circle.

1 I **waited / was waiting** for Mum
  when I **saw / was seeing** the accident.

2 When it **started / was starting** to rain,
  we **walked / were walking** home.

3 He **played / was playing** the piano
  when his friends **arrived / were arriving**.

4 When I **tidied / was tidying** my room,
  I **found / was finding** some money.

5 Police!

Used to

> They **used to live** near us.   That cat **used to sleep** in its basket!

Make sentences.

1 cream / Mum / love / used / ice / to

   _____

2 used / hamsters / have / we / to / two

   _____

3 sister / long / used / my / have / hair / to

   _____

4 parents / live / my / used / in / to / America

   _____

5 be / Grandpa / to / a / officer / used / police

   _____

Had to

> My dad **had to go** to school on Saturdays.
> The cat **had to sleep** in its basket last night.

Complete the sentences. Use *had to* and the words from the box.

> tidy   do   run   get up

1 We _____ very early for the plane.
2 I _____ my room at the weekend.
3 They _____ fast to catch the bus.
4 He _____ a lot of homework yesterday.

⑥ Mythical beasts

Comparatives and superlatives

My bike's **faster than** your bike.
Paul is **better** at Maths **than** me.
We were **worse than** the other team.
Music is **more interesting than** Art.
Why is my school bag **heavier** today?

It's **the fastest** train in the world.
My dad's **the best** driver in the world.
It was **the worst** day of my life.
History is **the most interesting** subject.
It's **the fattest** cat in town!

1 Complete the sentences.

1 I'm _____ _____ you at Science. (bad)

2 Dan is _____ _____ boy in our class. (silly)

3 You're _____ _____ mum in the world. (good)

4 I'm two days _____ _____ my best friend. (old)

5 It's _____ _____ _____ computer game
   in the world! (exciting)

It looks like ...

What **do** zebras **look like**?
What **does** your sister **look like**?
What **does** your cat **look like**?

They **look like** black and white horses.
She's got long brown hair and blue eyes.
It usually **looks like** it's hungry!

1 Make sentences.

1 do / like / look / what / pandas / ?

   _____

2 the / what / like / Phoenix / look / does / ?

   _____

3 does / friend / best / like / look / your / what / ?

   _____

7 Orchestra practice

Possessive pronouns

> It's **my** bag. = It's **mine**.   It's **your** bag. = It's **yours**.
> It's **his** bag. = It's **his**.   It's **her** bag. = It's **hers**.
> It's **our** bag. = It's **ours**.   It's **their** bag. = It's **theirs**.

1 Complete the sentences.

1 Tim and Fred, is this your dog?
   No, it isn't _____ .

2 Is this my hat?
   Yes, Grandpa. That's _____ .

3 Is this Sue's coat? Yes, it's _____ .

4 Is this your cat, Mike? Yes, it's _____ .

5 Is this George and Henry's house?
   No, _____ is the big house over there.

who / which / where

> Dan's the boy **who** plays the guitar.
> The pen **which** I lost is blue.
> The house **where** Tabby lives has got a small garden.

1 Complete the sentences.

1 Gina is the girl _____ sits next to me.

2 The town _____ we live is near the sea.

3 The skateboard _____ I want costs £40.

4 Is he the boy _____ plays the trumpet?

5 Where's the cake _____ Grandma made?

6 This is the hall _____ we practise.

8 In the planetarium

Will

> You'll (You **will**) **be** famous one day.
> What **will** you **be** when you grow up?
> **Will** it **be** difficult?
>
> They'll (They **will**) **visit** the moon.
> I'll (I **will**) **be** an astronaut.
> Don't worry. It'll (It **will**) **be** easy.

1 Rewrite the sentences with 'll.

1 I will be a teacher.

_____

2 They will be very happy.

_____

3 It will rain next week.

_____

4 He will be an actor.

_____

5 We will visit other planets.

_____

Adverbs

> He shouted **angrily**.
> The alien spoke very **slowly**.
>
> Our class did the test **badly**.
> The cat sang **loudly** all night.

1 Write the adverbs to complete the sentences.

1 Please come _____ . (quick)

2 She paints _____ . (beautiful)

3 The baby smiled _____ . (happy)

4 Our teacher talks very _____ . (quiet)

5 That UFO's flying _____ . (dangerous)

At the campsite

a bottle / can / loaf / packet / piece of

 a bottle of milk

 a packet of biscuits

 **two loaves of** bread

 a loaf of bread

 a can of lemonade

 a piece of cake

Can I have some milk?

Complete the phrases.

 1 a _____ of cheese

 2 a _____ of crisps

 3 a _____ of apple juice

 4 a _____ of pears

How much? / How many?

How much water do we need?   **How many** bottles of water do we need?

How much bread do we need?   **How many** loaves of bread do we need?

How much milk do we need?   **How many** eggs do we need?

 ## Complete the questions.

1 How _____ carrots do we need?
2 How _____ cheese do we need?
3 How _____ packets of crisps do we need?
4 How _____ bottles of juice do we need?
5 How _____ oranges do we need?

Thanks and acknowledgements

Authors' thanks

We would like to thank our editorial team very warmly: Aldona Gawlinski, Liane Grainger and Bridget Kelly. You have worked extremely hard and with a lot of dedication to make this course a success. It was a pleasure working with you on this project. Thank you for your commitment, and for your great sense of humour!

We would also like to thank Maria Pylas, Associate Publishing Director, for many interesting discussions and for choosing us as the author team for this project. It's been a great experience, Maria!

The publishers are grateful to the following contributors:

Pippa Mayfield: freelance editor
Oliver Design: concept design
Pentacorbig and Blooberry: cover design, book design and page make-up
Hilary Fletcher: picture research
John Green and Tim Woolf, TEFL Tapes: audio recordings
Robert Lee: song writing

Special thanks to Kay Bentley and Robert Quinn for their contribution in the development of the 'English for school' sections of the Student's Book.

Special thanks to Karen Elliott for developing the phonics material.

The publishers and authors would like to thank the following teachers and reviewers for their help in developing the course:

Argentina: Liliana Amado, María Silvia Caride, Gabriela Finkelstein, Susana Lagier, Gladys Ledwith, María Sol Luppi, Mónica Marinakis, Silvia Miranda, Natalia Monty, Pamela Pogré, Adriana Raffo, Viviana Rondina, Inés Salomón, Stella Maris Schulte, María Teresa de Vido de Stringa, María Marta Taurozzi
Chile: Sandra Durán Vega, Fernanda Tornero
Egypt: Nabil Ezz-el Deen, Iglal El Gamel, Ghada Farouk, Nemat Matta, Sonia Abdul Rahman, Daniel Rolph, Amy Sarkiss
Mexico: Claudia Mejía Escalante, Lucia García, Imelda Calderón Gómez, Laura Landa Herrera, Yeymi Ortiz Iberra, Claudia Camacho Jiménez, Rosa María Martínez Maldonado, José Antonio Martínez, Guadalupe Mejía, María Teresa Moguel, María del Rosario Limón Ortiz, María Teresa Patrón, Yara Gil Pérez, Lorena Sánchez Pérez, Ivette Portales, Yolanda Gómez Saldana, Diana Naim Sucar
Spain: Arantxa Abalos, Julius Krajewski, Ángela McClenaghan, Ken O'Carroll, Noreen O'Donnell, John West, Valerie Weston
Turkey: Deniz Altiparmak, Lisa Broomhead, Celia Gasgil
UK: Lucy Frino, Pippa Mayfield, Susannah Reed, Hilary Ratcliff, Melanie Williams

The publishers are grateful to the following illustrators:

Alan Rowe, Andy Parker, Anna Hancock (The Illustrators Agency), Ben Hasler (NB Illustration), Bernice Lum, Bill Ledger, Brenda McKetty (Beehive Illustration), Christina Forshay (The Bright Agency), Dan Chernett (The Bright Agency), Hannah Radenkova (The Bright Agency), Iva Sasheva (The Bright Agency), James Elston (Sylvie Poggio Artists), Katriona Chapman (The Bright Agency), Marek, Mark Duffin, Martin Sanders (Beehive Illustration), Sam Church, Savi (The Apple Agency)

The authors and publishers acknowledge the following sources of copyright material and are grateful for the permissions granted. While every effort has been made, it has not always been possible to identify the sources of all the material used, or to trace all copyright holders. If any omissions are brought to our notice, we will be happy to include the appropriate acknowledgements on reprinting.

Key: l = left, c = centre, r = right, t = top, b = bottom.

p. 18 (IL): Alamy/© World Pictures; p. 18 (IR): Alamy/© Robert Harding Picture Library Ltd; p. 18 (2L): Alamy/© The Art Archive; p. 18 (2CL): Alamy/© The Art Archive; p. 18 (2CR): Shutterstock Images/Maugli; p. 18 (2R): Shutterstock Images/Irafael; p. 18 (B/G): Thinkstock/Photodisc; p. 19 (4BL): Shutterstock/Oleksiy Mark; p. 19 (4BR): Shutterstock/Lusoimages; p. 19 (4TR): Shutterstock/John Kasawa; p 19 (4TL): Shutterstock Images/Chiyacat; p. 19 (B/G): Thinkstock/Stockbyte; p. 23: Shutterstock Images/Kosoff; p. 24 (B/G): Thinkstock/Comstock; p. 24 (R): Thinkstock/iStockphoto; p. 30 (TL): Sunday Afternoon on the Island of La Grande Jatte, 1884-86 (oil on canvas) by Seurat, Georges Pierre (1859-91). The Art Institute of Chicago, IL, USA/ The Bridgeman Art Library. Nationality / copyright status: French / out of copyright; p. 30 (BL): © Ezshwan Winding www.ezshwan.com; p. 30 (TR): Getty Images/Gamma-Rapho/Raphael Gaillarde; p. 30 (BR): ©The National Gallery 2011/A River Landscape by Joris van der Haagen (about 1615-1669). Oil on canvas. Bequeathed by Mrs Jewer Henry Jewer, 1873; p. 30-31 (B/G): Thinkstock/iStockphoto; p. 36 (B/G): Thinkstock/iStockphoto; p. 42-43 (B/G): Thinkstock/AbleStock.com; p. 48 (B/G): Thinkstock/iStockphoto; p. 54 (2TL): Getty Images/Stone/Steve Bronstein; p. 54 (2CL): Alamy/© isifa Image Service s.r.o.; p. 54 (2CR): Shutterstock Images/Andre Blais; p. 54 (2R): Shutterstock Images/Christian Lagerek; p. 54 (IL): Photodisc/Henrik Weis; p. 54 (IR): SuperStock Images/©Corbis; p. 54-55 (B/G): Thinkstock/Digital Vision; p. 60 (B/G): Thinkstock/iStockphoto; p. 66 (TL): Rex Features/Everett Collection; p. 66 (TR): Rex Features/Roger-Viollet; p. 66 (BL): Rex Features/Everett Collection; p. 66 (CR): Kobal Collection/20th Century Fox; p. 66 (BR): Rex Features; p. 66-67 (B/G): Shutterstock Images/Bruce Rolff; p. 67: Rex Features/Everett Collection; p. 68 (IL): from Double Act by Jacqueline Wilson, published by Corgi Yearling. Reprinted by permission of The Random House Group Limited; p. 68 (IR): From George and the Big Bang by Lucy and Stephen Hawking, published by Doubleday. Reprinted by permission of The Random House Group Ltd; p. 78 (I): Corbis/©Keren Su; p. 78 (2TL): Getty Images/Federico Veronesi; p. 78 (2TR): Getty Images/Visuals Unlimited, Inc./Leroy Simon; p. 78 (2BL): Photolibrary.com/Peter Arnold Images/ Martin Harvey; p. 78 (2BR): Photolibrary.com/Peter Arnold Images/ Martin Harvey; p. 78-79 (B/G): Thinkstock/Photodisc; p. 79 (IL): iStockphoto/tilo; p. 79 (ICL): iStockphoto/rontography; p. 79 (ICR): iStockphoto/stedenmi; p. 79 (IR): Photolibrary.com/All Canada Photos/ Wayne Lynch; p. 88 (L): Shutterstock Images/Scott E Read; p. 88 (CL): iStockphoto/KeithSzafranski; p. 88 (C): Shutterstock Images/Michael Woodruff; p. 88 (CR): Alamy/© David Osborn; p. 88 (R): Shutterstock Images/ArvydasS; p. 90 (B/G): Thinkstock/iStockphoto; p. 102 (I): Getty Images/the Agency Collection/Stocktrek Images; p. 102-103 (B/G): Thinkstock/iStockphoto; p. 108 (B/G): Thinkstock/Flonline; p. 109 (I eggs): Shutterstock Images/Evgeny Karandaev; p. 109 (I juice): Shutterstock Images/Evgeny Karandaev; p. 109 (I cheese): Shutterstock Images/Edyta Pawlowska; p. 109 (I bread): Shutterstock Images/aarrows; p. 109 (I crisps): Shutterstock Images/Ewa Walicka; p. 109 (I chocolate): Shutterstock Images/Lasse Kristensen; p. 109 (I tomato): Shutterstock Images/Fedorov Oleksiy; p. 114-115: Thinkstock/iStockphoto.

Commissioned photography by: Stephen Bond p. 11, 20, 25, 44, 47, 48, 55 (1, 2), 56, 68 (2), 80, 83, 90, 91, 97, 104, 116.